DONALD JACKSON
KING OF BLADES

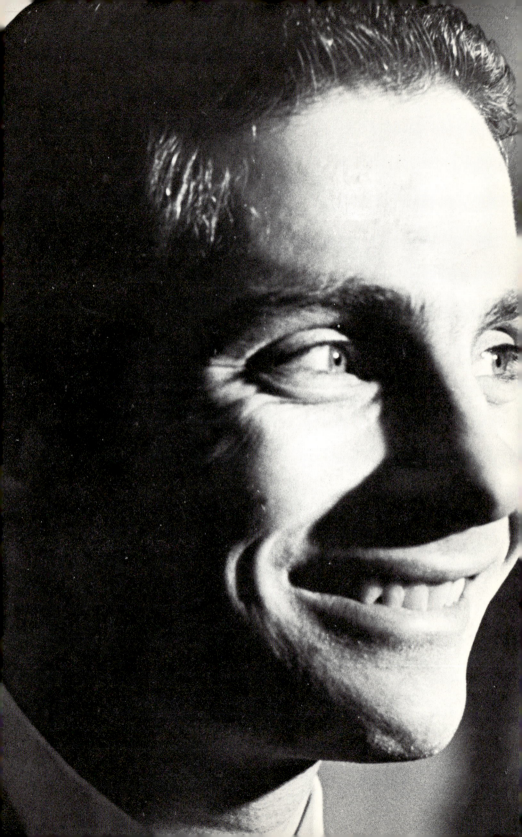

DONALD JACKSON
KING OF BLADES

by
GEORGE GROSS

QUEEN CITY PUBLISHING LTD.
TORONTO - CANADA

Gross, George.
   Donald Jackson — King of Blades

ISBN 0-9690508-1-X

1. Jackson, Donald, 1940–   2. Skaters —
Biography.

GV850.J32G76   796.9′1′0924   C77-001574-3

1 2 3 4 5 6 7 8 9 80 79 78 77

QUEEN CITY PUBLISHING LTD.
Box 369 - Station Z
Toronto - Ontario - Canada
M5N 2Z5

Dedication

To my wife Elizabeth, daughter Teddy and son George Junior, without whose help this book would not have been possible.

Preface

It was in the winter of 1959 that I first met Donald Jackson. I was assigned by The Toronto Telegram to cover the North American Figure Skating Championships and became interested in the impressive free-skating style of this young man from Oshawa.

Trailing Tim Brown and Robert Lee Brewer of the United States following the compulsory figures, the gutsy and superbly-talented performer turned defeat into victory with a stunning free-skating performance that swept him into first place and a standing ovation from the fans at Varsity Arena.

From then on I followed his career very closely not only as a journalist, but also as a friend. I got to know his parents well and was fascinated by the dedication of the entire family to help young Donald become a successful skater. I was, of course, just as impressed with his determination to overcome all obstacles to reach his goal — a gold medal at the World Championships.

The thought of writing a book about him was in the back of my mind for a long time. But I didn't tackle it in earnest until one day I chatted with Don, his manager Max Gould and another friend, Dr. Sidney Soanes. Sidney had published a book on ice dancing and showed great interest in publishing a book on Don Jackson.

After a few meetings it was decided we'd go ahead with a book on the fellow who came up with one of the greatest come-from-behind efforts in the annals of Canadian sports.

August 1977   **George Gross**

Acknowledgements

To my son George Junior for doing most of the work.

To the National Film Board for permission to use the title *Donald Jackson — King of Blades*. Also for supplying the Triple Lutz pictures.

To Candid Productions Inc., Dick Button, President, for permission to use frames of the Triple Lutz performance.

To the United States Figure Skating Association and to *Skating* Magazine for the loan of several photographs.

To Dennis Bird for the background material.

To the Toronto Telegram for the photograph of the Frontispiece.

To all those photographers whom we didn't credit with their photographs because we received them without indication of source.

To Sidney Soanes for the cover design; cover photograph of Donald Jackson by Daniel G. Neuman, Ice Photo Studio.

To Ross Tedder of Graphic Reproductions for his technical advice.

To Jim Proudfoot, Jim Coleman, Dick Button and Alan Weeks for reviewing the book.

G.G.

Foreword

Skating has been good to me. It has brought me many things I value and cherish. I have been fortunate in finding good friends. George Gross is high on that list.

I first met George in the winter of 1959 when I was a competitor in the North American Championships and George was covering the event for the Toronto Telegram. He was one of a small group of knowledgeable sportswriters who brought figure skating onto the sports pages of our newspapers.

After a career with the Toronto Telegram George became sports editor of The Toronto Sun in 1971. In 1973 he was an Ontario Sports Achievement Award winner, topping that by winning the National Newspaper Award for sportswriting the following year. In 1975 he received the Sports Federation of Canada award and in 1976 a special award for coverage of the Summer Olympic Games in Montreal.

I have great respect for George and his knowledge of skating. He has the knack of imparting it. He's a warm, considerate and compassionate person, and a friend I can trust.

George retained his interest in my career even after I won the World Championship. It was a happy day for me when he sat down to write my story. We hope it will help skaters and athletes in all sports to reach their goals.

Although skaters are on their own when the time comes to step on the ice before judges, competitive skating is very much a behind-the-scenes team effort. No one can do it alone.

So, starting with my parents who sacrificed much to keep me going, and including the professionals who taught me, the judges who judged me, the media people who wrote and talked about me, and the friends who encouraged me, to these people I extend my heartfelt thanks.

August 1977   **Donald Jackson**

Contents

The "movie" of the Triple Lutz begins on page 3.
A list of Don's major awards begins on page 153.

Prologue

Don Jackson's eyes slowly flickered open in reaction to the sunlight that had just begun creeping in over the sill of his bedroom window. He glanced at the alarm clock, which showed it was 5:50. He reached over and shut off the alarm before it could ring, leaned over and gave his wife Joanne a kiss and then slid noiselessly out of bed.

As he dressed, Don smiled. It was just like his amateur days all over again. Only the place and his role were different. Now he went down to the kitchen and made his own breakfast unlike years before when he was young and unknown, and his mother had always been up first in the Jackson household.

After putting the dishes away, Don went into the living room to pick up his skates and notes which were lying on the couch by the window. As he turned to leave, his eyes swept round the room. Memories came flooding back to him. There was a picture of Sydney, Australia, that he had received for a show there. On the far wall was a painting of the skyline in Prague, given in appreciation of a show and clinic. In a mahogany cabinet was a glass sculpture with four white horses embedded in it. The horses, depicted with wings, seemed ready to fly as the sun's rays burst back from them through the glass casing. On top of the cabinet stood another glass sculpture, a figure in a forward lean with arms extended in front and back, and knees deeply bent, awarded to him after another performance he had given in Prague fifteen years earlier. But there was no time

1

to think about it right now. He grabbed his skates, notes and a letter he had received two days before and left the house.

It took about twenty minutes to drive to the arena. There, his pupil was waiting to go on the ice. He was about to greet her and her mother when a friend came up and interrupted.

"Hey, Don! Heard the great news yesterday. Max said you'd bring the letter with you. May I read it?"

"Sure." Don reached for the letter and handed it over. His friend read the date, June 1st, 1977, and:

> Dear Donald,
>
> On behalf of the United States Figure Skating Association, I am honored to inform you of your election to its Figure Skating Hall of Fame, which was officially announced on the occasion of the recent annual meeting of the Association in Oakland, California.
>
> Election to the USFSA Hall of Fame brings with it the distinction of being ranked among those whose contribution to the sport of figure skating has been most outstanding. Nominations are made by the public at large and are voted on by a panel of distinguished electors who represent the figure skaters of the world.
>
> . . . In addition, your picture and name will be placed on permanent display in the Hall of Fame section of the USFSA Museum. . . .
>
> We, in the USFSA are most pleased that your accomplishments in and contribution to the sport of figure skating have been duly recognized by your election to the Hall of Fame. . . .

"It must be like a dream come true," the friend said. Don nodded, smiling broadly. Certainly there had been a dream come true. However, it was not this latest honour, though he did value it highly. Really, though, the dream

To see the famous Triple Lutz
from Don's 1962 World
Championship program flip
the pages like this:

was represented by that glass figure on the mahogany cabinet at home—leaning forward in a position ready to jump. His life on skates, caught in glass. . . .

Don laced up his skates. His student came slowly over to where he sat. She stood waiting until he glanced up and smiled at her. She hesitated slightly before saying: "Mr. Jackson, what did you have to do to get put into a Hall of Fame?"

The question almost made him laugh. Instead, he smiled from ear to ear.

"Dream a little and work a lot," he murmured, almost to himself. But that was by no means the whole story. . . .

George, Pat and Donald Jackson

Donald Jackson—1 year old

Donald Jackson—Public School Carnival—February 1949—8 years old

1
Pat and George

". . . and do you, Patricia Matthews, take . . ." The minister's words trailed off into the distance for Alice Gray. She thought back to the day, three years earlier, when she and Pat Matthews had noticed a small but well-built man walking placidly along the other side of the street. She also recalled clearly Pat's seemingly idle statement to the effect that there walked the type of man she could marry. There was no reason to attribute any importance to the reaction; neither of them had ever seen the man before and didn't expect to, again.

". . . and do you, George Jackson, take . . ." The words jolted Alice back to the present. She stared with a smile at the man to whom the minister's remarks were directed. They had not even spoken to him on that day three years before. Yet there he stood next to the woman who had singled him out across a street.

The smile grew into a laugh as Alice made her way over to the newlyweds to congratulate them and remind Pat— now Pat Jackson—of the fairy-tale-like nature of this marriage. The reminder brought a girlish giggle to Pat's pretty but determined-looking face while George, her choice as husband, wryly remarked that it was clear to him he'd never had a chance all along; everything had been decided for him.

However, the year was 1935. What hadn't been decided for him was where he was going to get the money to start raising the family that he and Pat both wanted. He worked at Robson Leather in Oshawa for less than forty cents an hour. Pat had been working for a lawyer for even less. These were the depression days.

The financial worry of raising a family turned quickly to the worry of ever being able to raise a family at all. A year later, Pat lost their first child after a few months of pregnancy. Their doctor said they might be able to have a child eventually but that they would have to wait at least three years before trying again. They did. In 1939, the doctor gave Pat the go ahead. This time there were still complications, but not serious ones. On April 2nd, 1940, Donald George Jackson was born. He was six weeks premature and weighed a mere four pounds, so he required extra care. Pat gave it lovingly. After six weeks she became concerned. A lump had formed on Don's groin. The doctor diagnosed a double hernia and told Pat and George that the hernia might heal itself but Don would have to wear a special truss to restrict movement and give the healing process a chance. A nice theory—but it didn't work. With the truss a hindrance to movement, Don did not take his first steps until 15 months. Once started, however, he became a whirlwind of activity. Though painful, the truss became a fact of life to him in the 2½ years he wore it, but then another hospital examination revealed that the hernia had not healed. The doctors suggested an operation to correct the condition. But they added that Don would never be able to perform any strenuous physical activities. The news came as a blow to both parents. Pat, now several months pregnant with their second son (to be named Bill), loved sports. George, a former competitive runner of distinction, had had fatherly visions of his first born son enjoying sports as much as he had. But they were to learn doctors can be wrong.

6

Pat had quit work to look after her two boys (Bill was two months old). And, after Don's successful operation May 28th, she had her hands full. Don had been a dynamo in his truss. Now he was a super-dynamo, preferring climbing trees and using beds and couches as trampolines to playing with toys. Once worried that he'd never live an athletic life, now they had to try to slow him down. However, it was clear they would not be able to restrict his blast furnace of energy.

The only time they could get Don to sit down was at meal time. Even at the table, he could not get enough, always wanting the most meat and the biggest piece of cake. His table antics led Pat to nickname him "Me First" after a comic book character of the time who had hundreds of arms and was always grabbing for everything in sight. Scarlet fever slowed Don down a little, before he was four. Sunday School at Simcoe Street United Church in Oshawa found him the world's champion fidgeter and twitcher; kindergarten at Centre Street Public School the same. Moving to the Mary Street Public School for Grade One, "Me First" proved his skills as a runner against his classmates, much to the delight of his father. However, it was the needlework of his mother that brought him his first honours.

Each year Oshawa children were invited to compete for the best costumes in certain specified categories as part of the annual Rotary Parade. Pat made a monarch butterfly costume, which won Don first place in the animal and insect category when he was just six. But, it was another costume competition a year and a half later that proved to be of great significance to the entire Jackson family.

7

In March of 1948, just before his 8th birthday, "Me First" came home from school, out of breath from running, to inform his mother that Mary Street was having a winter carnival. A costume competition was part of the festivities. But there was a hitch. Each child was expected to appear on skates—a routine request as most Canadian children owned skates by the time they were eight years of age and in Grade Three. Yet, at that stage, "Me First" had never even been on skates much less having a pair of his own.

Pat asked around the neighbourhood. She was able to borrow a pair of hockey skates so that Don could appear in the carnival wearing the snowman costume which she had sewn for him. Barely able to stand erect, Don won the award for the best comic costume as the carnival got under way. Later, each class had skating races—and Don's ineptness on blades kept him from competing. That did not sit well with "Me First". Home from the carnival, Don told his mother he was going to learn to skate and win that race next year. The request soon took on more serious overtones. Less than a month later, George took his family to Toronto to see the Barbara Ann Scott Skating Show. Sitting in the stands enjoying the show, "Me First" suddenly sat up on the edge of his seat. His mouth was open in awe as he watched the swift but graceful free skating routine performed by the show's male star Don Tobin. No sooner had Tobin accepted his applause and left the ice surface, when "Me First" turned to his parents and said: "I don't want to just learn how to skate, I want to skate like *that!*"

Aware of his ambitious tendencies no matter what the issue, and realising that summer was upon them, Pat and George simply nodded assent and put it out of their minds. But skating was not going to be forgotten over the summer by "Me First".

In the midst of a summer heat wave, Don was walking by the creek near his home when he encountered a neigh-

bourhood lad a few years his senior, David Lowery. The two began to talk about sports. David mentioned that he was a member of the Oshawa Skating Club. Don's ears pricked up and David found himself deluged with a torrent of questions concerning the Club and learning how to skate.

After listening to Don's enthusiastic barrage, David (who later went on to become Canadian Junior Pairs Champion) advised him to keep after his parents to let him join the Club because it was the only place locally to pursue skating in any serious way. Don took the message home. Scarcely a day went by that he didn't ask to join the Skating Club. After talking with David, Pat and George decided to enrol Don in the winter session of 1948. They bought him a pair of girls' figure skates. Because of that, "Me First's" skating career almost did not get started. He took one look at the "sissy skates" and declared that he would never skate in anything like them. A quick paint job by George changed the image of the skates sufficiently so that, in September, Don was ready and willing to start the long haul toward fulfilling his initial dream.

His first few encounters with the ice were of a very timid nature. Unsure of himself on the slippery surface, Don clung to the boards, shuffling around the rink trying to establish a correct sense of balance. It didn't take him long. With Pat watching patiently from the stands, "Me First" one day called for her attention and thrust himself away from the boards. "Look, mom, I can *skate!*" he called. Pat smiled with pride as she watched her son stumble forward in little spurts. She also noticed that day the huge ear-to-ear grin that was never to leave Don's face while he was a competitive skater. Yet, what struck Pat the most was the determination she saw written behind the smile.

Less than two months later, the Club held its annual Christmas skating party. Among other things, there were age group races for the youngsters. Being eight and a half, Don had to skate in the eight to eleven classification, giving away much in size, strength and experience to the older boys in his age bracket. Still, he was the first one to the starting line when his race was called. The instant the race started, he burst out into a lead which he never relinquished. Pat and George sat in the stands not able to bask in the usual parental pride due to their intense state of shock.

Later, they decided to give Don one figure skating lesson per week with the club pro, Nan Unsworth, who was charging seventy-five cents for fifteen minutes at that time. Also, Don continued with the group lessons which he had been taking with Alex Fulton. It was mainly through the games that Alex employed in the huge group lessons that Don learned how to skate. Group lessons were the only viable means of teaching a lot of kids at once in a club the size of Oshawa's. Being the only big skating club between Toronto and Ottawa, the club had upwards of 350 members in its programmes.

In group lessons, Alex employed a series of obstacle courses at which Don quickly became the most adept. Don also quickly learned to skate backwards. This, and his obstacle course ability, won him a skating role in the club's annual winter carnival—as a runaway baby.

This honour inspired Don to look for extra ice time anywhere he could find it. On winter weekends, Pat and George often took Don and his brother Bill up to their aunt's frozen pond to skate. Pat also took Don around to various school rinks. One day she watched Don practise a two-footed spin which he had learned at the club. His simple manoeuvre caused all the other children to stop their skating to watch —a fact which raised a deep feeling of pride in Pat.

Don practised his role diligently for the big day of the performance at the carnival ice show. However, sickness once again set him back. In February, Don was hospitalized after contracting pneumonia, which caused him to miss the carnival and the first role he had ever earned. It was a bad winter in other ways. Pat, George and Bill all wound up in hospital during the next few months with different types of pulmonary infections.

Without any hospitalization plans at that time to assist him financially, George was forced to sell some land he had bought under the Veteran's Land Act in order to meet the backbreaking cost of four successive convalescences. Concerned over the cause of the infection to the entire family, he decided that it must be due to something at the rink which was the only place at which the entire family constantly spent time. The doctor in charge sensed George's concern about the rink and its effects and quickly told him not to let such a theory deter Don's skating. Summer was nearing. Rest and warm weather would help them all.

During that summer of '49, Don's attention turned to track and field, and cub scouts. Although he had outgrown the "Me First" label, he hadn't outgrown the ambitious attitude that caused it. He began to win consistently the running races in which he was entered.

It was none too soon for Don, however, when fall rolled around bringing with it the start of another skating season at the club. After careful deliberation concerning finances and Don's ability and seriousness, Pat and George decided to increase his private figure lessons by one and to add one private free skating lesson each week. The news sent Don into seventh heaven as it meant an increased opportunity to improve.

The previous year, Don had had difficulty understanding the nature of figures and why he had to go around in circles for fifteen minutes in a small area rather than trying to skate freely all over the ice. With the one free skating lesson, he now had his chance. But it made the figure skating lesson which immediately preceded it seem endless. He continually stole glances at the wall clock waiting for the time that would both signal an end to that lesson and the start of his free skating session.

By the early part of winter, he was again recognized by the club directors and given a lead in the club's Ice Frolics show. Practising hard once more, he was determined not to get sick again and have to miss the show. But boys love to play. Less than a month after receiving the role, Don was playing tag. Chasing a girl off the ice he ran head first into a cross bar that had been left across an exit. Dazed, he crumpled to the ice, blood trickling down his forehead. The frightened scream of the girl he had been chasing alerted one of the pros to the accident. Rather than attend to the wound, he pulled Don to his feet and made him go out and attempt to skate. It was a theory often followed after an ice accident—you jump up instantly and go at it again.

Whether a knock on the head could have kept Don out of skating, the way he felt about it, was unlikely. Anyway, he was back on the ice skating the next day as if nothing had happened.

Just after that incident, Don celebrated his tenth birthday and prepared to enter his first figure skating competition. This was a novice event held within the Oshawa Skating Club. As had been the case in the races a year before, he showed no signs of nervous unrest as the day of competition approached.

For the competition, each skater was required to go out

onto the ice and skate as he or she pleased for two minutes to the music provided. The tune that started as Don's turn came up was the Red Barn Polka and, instead of stopping after the required two minutes, he just kept going until the music had ended. During his improvised routine, he attempted to do the simple two-foot spin he had done so well during the winter at the school skating rinks. However, as he went into the position for the spin, his legs slid along the ice until they seemed to lock in a crossed position. Unwilling to stop once he had started and, employing his great natural sense of balance, Don held onto the stance as he slowly spun around.

The older skaters watched in surprise. They realised that he was doing a difficult crossed-foot spin and shouted to him to keep going. Oblivious to the nature of his accomplishment and grateful for the advice and encouragement he was receiving, he kept going as long as he was able to maintain the momentum for the spin. He finished up skating with that characteristic smile of total enjoyment all over his face—a smile that returned soon after when he found out that he had won the Tonkin Trophy which was emblematic of novice supremacy in the club.

The victory soon took a backseat to the preparations for the Ice Frolics show in March. Don knew his role by heart and performed well in front of his first audience, which naturally included Pat, George and Bill. Pat, always with the warm smile as she watched her son skate, turned to George and remarked how healthy their son looked as he sped merrily around the ice dressed in the ringmaster's outfit. Don, wrapped up in the excitement of the show, had

Don wins his first trophy—Tonkin Trophy
—Novice Championship, Oshawa Skating
Club

The Snake Charmer—Oshawa SC Carnival,
1952

Little Boy Blue — Oshawa Skating Club
Carnival, 1951

Don as Ringmaster in the Oshawa SC
Carnival—girls L to R: Gloria Tatton,
Gracie Dow, Joan Kelly, Carol Klapow

forgotten about the excessive heat he was experiencing throughout his body.

The next morning, much to Pat's dismay, the doctor had to be called in to see Don who had awakened in a pool of sweat. His diagnosis confirmed the fact that Don had skated with a high fever the night before. He had the mumps and would be in bed for at least a week. The news upset Don even more than the sickness as it meant he would have to miss the upcoming skating tests at the club.

Once he had recovered, Don began to work even harder at all his lessons until, a month later, he was deemed ready by his pro (Nan Unsworth) to attempt his first level figure test. This was the initial rung on the ladder leading to qualification for national and international competition. Unknown to anyone at the time, it was to be but the first in a long line of such attempts. Don's very small and slight build made it extra difficult for him to create an impression on the ice from which he could trace his figure.

Two of the three judges involved in evaluating the tests that day were Dick and Patsy McLaughlin. Both had considerable experience in skating and judging. Dick was the President of the Club. Later, he became the President of the Canadian Figure Skating Association. Competitively, he had won the Canadian Junior Championship while Patsy had been second in the Senior Championship.

Dick and Patsy both quickly recognized Don's great talent for skating, watching the fluid movements of his body as it glided over the ice. To them, however, basic figures were of the utmost importance in skating. As a result, they failed Don on that test attempt—a fact that did not seem to bother him much, but that disappointed his parents.

Before their disappointment had time to influence any decisions they might make concerning Don's career in skating, Nan Unsworth convinced Pat and George that their son had the ability to become a Canadian champion. She said they should seriously consider sending him to a summer skating school for extra work and instruction.

Cobourg was opening a summer skating school at the time. Nan was one of the instructing professionals. Pat therefore began to inquire in Cobourg for places where Don might stay for four weeks—the time she and George had decided they could afford. They found a room with Dave Carr and his wife, but driving home to Oshawa George voiced second thoughts about the family's ability to bear the financial burden of four weeks' room and board plus skating fee. Pat tried to convince him that the sacrifice was worth it. Still talking, they entered their house. The phone rang. It was the Cobourg operator, for Mrs. George Jackson. Pat answered. Dave Carr was on the line. She thought at first there'd been a hitch—that the Carrs had changed their mind. It was the opposite: a solution to their financial problems. Dave stated that if she would come to Cobourg for the summer to help with house-keeping and cooking meals for the skaters, she and Don could both stay there free of charge. No more financial strain! Don would now be able to stay for eight weeks instead of four! "I'll be there!" she said.

Throughout that summer, she scrubbed floors, washed dishes and cooked meals so that Don could skate. Twice again during the summer Don tried his first-level figure test. Twice more he failed. At this point, Pat and George (who drove up to Cobourg with Bill whenever possible) began to despair. If Don couldn't pass his first test, how could he ever hope to become even a decent figure skater, let alone Canadian champion? However, Pat's belief in her son overrode the doubts. She attempted to bolster Don's confidence

16

by telling him that she had told the judges that he was serious about competitive skating and that she and George did not want the judges just "giving" him a pass to push him ahead.

At that time, Dick McLaughlin was busy negotiating with one of the top skaters in the world to come to Canada and become the chief pro at the Oshawa Skating Club. When the deal was finally concluded, Dick posted the news to the members of the club. The notice said that, in order to take lessons from the new pro, families would have to pre-sign their children to a special list. When it was full, no more applications would be accepted.

Pat immediately put Don's name on the list. Although she didn't know it at the time, the new pro was to have a major, perhaps the greatest influence on the skating style and attitude of her son not only then but throughout the entire length of his career. . . .

Ede Kiraly with Don at Cobourg—Summer 1951

2

Ede

In choosing Hungarian-born Ede Kiraly as the new pro at the Oshawa Skating Club, Dick McLaughlin had gone for the best. Only a year previously, at the 1949 World Championships, Kiraly had come the closest of any male skater in history to performing the unbelievable feat of capturing the gold medal in both the singles and pairs competition. He'd placed second in the singles after capturing the world title in the pairs. He'd been a trend setter in both events as well. In the pairs, he and his partner were first to execute the overhead axel lift.

Yet, even more important than his impressive record was his attitude towards skating. This attitude, projected by a truly unselfish coaching philosophy, soon was to be deeply reflected in Don Jackson.

Full of enthusiasm for his new job, Ede received a shock only days after his arrival into the Oshawa area. Pat had immediately jumped at the opportunity to sign Don to Ede's teaching list. But perhaps due to Ede's fees for lessons being higher than others, few in the club had done likewise. In Canada for only a few days and speaking little English, he didn't know what to think or do. However, when he skated onto the ice at the Oshawa Arena a short time later, he quit worrying. Though the club members had been hesitant, skaters from Burlington, Toronto, Ottawa and other areas had jumped at the chance. He was booked solid.

At first Don was just another pupil to Ede, taking one figure and one free skating lesson a week. But soon Ede realized that the small, light ten-year-old had great natural ability. The more he watched, the surer he became: this boy had a chance for international greatness. With that conviction, he laid out a coaching plan in his own mind. Its working title, quite simply, was: The Development of Don Jackson as Future Champion of the World. His approach would necessarily mean fewer immediate results—a difficult position for a coach when parents are looking for results. But this was a special coach and these were special parents. They were behind their son's participation as long as he was enjoying what he was doing. It was to this attitude—enjoyment—that Ede first applied himself.

Ede's love for the sport had made his life, brought him fame, travel, happiness. He never failed to project his sense of enjoyment to his pupils. The message was, "Aren't we lucky to be doing what we love doing, and doing it better every day?" Don responded. That was his natural way, too. His smile grew broader and broader with each lesson, especially when he began to progress—and what a progression! By the end of the first half season of skating with Ede, he had learned every single jump including the lutz. Ede felt he was now ready to try and accomplish an axel jump.

With the technical influence of some of the famous European coaches such as Arnold Gerschwiler behind him, Ede spent the first lesson using their "work-up" approach to try to teach Don the axel. With great care he explained the jump, breaking it down into attempts at a half turn, then at a full turn, finally getting to the full jump with its one and a half turns in the air.

With only a couple of minutes remaining in the lesson, Ede saw that Don, eager as he was, was completely lost,

and no further ahead than he had been before the lesson had started. Greatly concerned, Ede decided to end the lesson by doing a few complete axels in order to show Don what he should expect to do soon.

Don watched. A broad smile broke across his face for the first time during the lesson as Ede sped down the ice and leaped into the air for the one and a half revolutions needed to complete the axel jump. When his coach had finished and was coming back to say, "That's all for today," Don skated to centre ice, picked up speed and leaped into the execution of a perfect axel! In Ede's total astonishment, he yelled across the arena to George, watching from the stands as usual, "Donald did an axel! A *perfect axel*! And on the very *first* try!" It was the single most important lesson for Ede. He now realised for the first time Don's extraordinary capacity to create mental images and transform them readily into complete movements. From then on Ede always knew that with Don a demonstration was worth more than a thousand words.

Though advancing quickly in free skating, Don was still having his problems with figures. Twice more he tried to pass the first level test and was unsuccessful both times. However, this time there was not the despair Pat and George had felt the previous summer. They, along with Don, now believed in the theory of coaching that Ede expounded to them.

Ede had the revolutionary idea of teaching figures in such a way as to help the free skating. He wanted to bring figures and free skating together to form a unit. Thus, in teaching Don the figures, Ede concerned himself not with the test requirement of the perfect tracing of a circle in itself, but rather with the proper form to create correct tracing and the creation of a true circle through proper lean.

Ede felt strongly that passing the First Test could wait as long as was necessary for Don to pass it using a technique of "feeling" the circle, thus overcoming his handicap of light tracing (due to his slight stature) by fine body control rather than visual dependency. Ede knew well the pain of failure. He had failed his own Third Test several times at a time when there were only three tests. (When he finally did pass the Third Test, the international governing body decided to introduce a Fourth Test which meant he would have to try all over again to gain international status!) Anyway, Ede's long-range planning for Don paid off much later in the development of the famous "Jackson footwork", made possible by Donald's mastery of fluid body movements in his early figures training.

During the winter of 1951, at about the time Don accomplished his first axel jump, Ede and senior coaches at the Granite Club in Toronto and the Hamilton Skating Club proposed to their club executives that an interclub competition be established. Novice and juvenile skaters needed competition at a level beyond that of the local Intraclub meet, they argued. Dick McLaughlin threw in full support from the Oshawa executive and the project was launched that same winter.

The Interclub meet marked the beginning of Don's competitive career. Being the youngest entrant (at 11) did not bother him any more than it had at the Oshawa club races. Against stiff, experienced competition from skaters several years older, he skated to a fifth place finish in the junior men's category.

A few weeks later, the winter skating season was coming to a close. Ede suggested to Pat and George that Don would greatly benefit from another summer of extra practice back at the Cobourg Summer School. As Ede would

be teaching there, they readily consented, finding the money once again from the tight family budget—partly because Pat had returned to work with Bill now old enough not to require constant supervision during the day.

Having passed his First Test on the seventh try, Don worked hard during the summer on the figures for the Second Test. Yet, this summer was to be more important because it gave Don his first experiences skating regularly for an audience. Every Sunday evening the arena provided a mixture of entertainment which included skating. The arena was a wonderful place to cool off after a hot summer's day. The performers often wondered to themselves whether it was the air conditioning or the entertainment that brought the people in each week. Don loved skating for the audience at the start of each show, and they very soon began to love him. His performance was entertaining and often unexpected. He kept the audience guessing—even as to how many times he would fall! There was fun in other ways. One night as Ede was warming up for his routine after Don had skated particularly well, Ede was startled somewhat when the master of ceremonies congratulated him on how well *his* son had skated!

After a brief layoff, Don and Ede returned to the Oshawa arena full of enthusiasm for the fall-winter skating season. After school, on weekends and early some mornings, Don worked hard on his figures. When he tried the Second Test for the first time, he failed. This time he was disappointed in himself as he judged his test to have been a good one. Pat and George tried comforting Don, assuring him he'd pass the next time. He didn't. And he missed a third time.

That time Pat broke down and cried. She could foresee

1952 Oshawa SC Club Champions. Standing L to R: Margaret Jean Carr, Hugh Smith, Toby Keeler, Dawn Steckley, David Lowery; seated: Don Petre, Mary Ellen Petre, Kathy Learmonth, Don Jackson, Junior Champion

Don and his father with some of Don's trophies

24

longer and longer lists of failures awaiting her son at each successive level. Ede gently reminded her and George that Don was making great progress in all other aspects of skating. He said this delay in passing his tests would be of invaluable service to Don's future career, by keeping him concentrating on the fundamentals while everything else developed at a fast clip.

With all the single jumps and the axel under his belt, it was time for Don to attempt a double loop jump. As the jumps had become more complicated, Ede's carefully planned coaching strategies had begun to play a bigger role in Don's skating development. Now Ede dispensed with analytical breakdowns of jumping and simply proceeded to impart knowledge directly to Don by demonstration. There were two things in jumping that bore the utmost importance in Ede's eyes—the rhythm the skater had as he approached the jump, and the height and distance he attained during the jump.

To Ede, everyone had natural body rhythm, but this had to be brought out. He skated miles up and down the rink as the weeks passed, manipulating Don's body in the rhythm needed for the jump. Not surprisingly, he found that Don picked up the rhythm very quickly and soon did not require any assistance in attaining the proper rhythm for himself before each jump.

With Ede's ample experience in lifting his pairs partner, it was a simple task for him to take Don as he approached a jump and catapult him forward and up into the air. To Don this was wonderful fun. After all, how many 12-year-olds have someone willing to help them fly far and long through the air several times every week? Even though returning to the ice was not always a soft landing.

Ede did not worry about the inconsistency that appeared in Don's early jumping. He knew why it existed. He also felt that the falls were a good learning experience for someone who had visions of becoming world champion. The inconsistency, Ede knew, was due to the fact that he had not insisted Don have perfect balance on takeoffs. He'd omitted this stress because he did not want Don—after all, still just a kid—to lose the excitement he had for skating, or reduce it to a chore, like figures. There would be plenty of time later on to develop consistency. Don, when older and more mature, would be able to maintain his feeling of excitement for the sport even in the face of restriction.

With his new found rhythm to help him, Don soon began to land his double loops perfectly . . . from time to time. Though not consistent, when the jumps did land, they were spectacular. Ede's coaching was paying off. Don got the chance to demonstrate his progress to the entire club when he was given a solo role in the annual Ice Frolics Show as a ringmaster.

Cracking a whip and skating from underneath oversized red boots, Don again won the hearts of an audience with the joy he projected. Pat and George sat proudly in the stands as they watched him race about the ice with that big smile on his face. Ede also smiled afterward when he overheard spectators remark that they had never seen anyone display such fast co-ordination and body reflexes while skating; a tribute both to Don, for having such skills, and to Ede for showing how they could best be used.

Then Ede received news that the famous European coach Arnold Gerschwiler was coming to Canada for a brief stay as an instructor at the Stratford Summer School. Unselfishly interested in Don's progress and therefore not one to try to keep his star pupil to himself, Ede convinced the Jacksons

to send Don to Stratford. Then he prevailed upon Arnold to give Don some basic figures instruction.

A strict disciplinarian, Arnold worked Don very hard. The atmosphere was one of a teaching monologue. This was very difficult for Don. He was mischievous. He had played such tricks during practice as offering hot-peppered chewing gum to Ede. Yet, it took only a few days before he accepted the idea of keeping silent during lessons. This was largely due to the fact that one day Arnold handed down an order that called upon Don to write "I must not talk on patch" two hundred times*. Later, when the paper was handed in, Arnold did not even glance at it but simply tore it to pieces and tossed it into the garbage.

Hard work on the figures soon paid large dividends. Don passed his Second Test. It was his fourth try, but first that summer. Pat never had to worry again. From then on, Don passed every successive level test the first time he tried it.

Arnold did not confine his instruction to figures. He noticed that Don had a fine double loop jump but it came off Don's right foot which was in opposition to his other jumps. He forced Don to re-learn the double loop on the other foot so it could be used in combination with other jumps. He also brought Don up another niche in the jumping hierarchy by teaching him the double salchow. Don was able to do it with clean take-offs and landings by the end of the summer.

Progressing rapidly now, even soaring, there was disheartening news for Don just ahead. The fall-winter skating season at the Oshawa club was about to start when Ede

---

*A "patch" is a small portion of the ice surface for a skater's own use for practicing figures.

27

announced that he would not return as club pro. Knowing that coaching could not be a lifelong career, Ede had trained in Europe as an engineer. Needing practical experience in Ontario in order to gain the status of a professional engineer, he had accepted an offer to work as an engineer in Peterborough.

Don had grown to love Ede. Ede's personality, his strong and athletic style of skating, had helped him through the long hours. Now, torn, he consented to let his father take him for a tryout in hockey. It was to be his first, last, and only.

When Don stepped on the ice at the hockey workout and started to skate, the coach of the team gasped. Don skated rings around every player there. He was always the first one to the puck. However, when it came to doing something with the puck once he had reached it, he was as bad as the least experienced player. His brother, Bill, more adept at puck-handling, made the team. Don went back where he belonged, to figure skating.

The new club pro was Wally Distelmeyer. Don took lessons as usual. Although the only new thing he learned during the year was a split jump, he enjoyed a measure of success in the regional Interclub competitions, the ones Ede had helped to start the previous year. In December of 1952, Don won the Interclub Novice championship at the Granite Club in Toronto. Two months later he repeated the feat at a meet in Hamilton.

In May of 1953, at 13, Don competed once more in the Oshawa club championships, this time easily winning the junior men's title for which he received the Victor trophy. Exhibiting his smile from ear to ear as he skated, he easily outdistanced his opponents with his performance. That night, however, he had an extra reason for his smile. He had just learned that Ede would be teaching at a summer skating school in Goderich.

Though eager to work again with Ede, Don almost never got the opportunity. George once again began to question the family's ability to bear the increasingly heavy expense. Pat's entire salary was going to pay for Don's skating. Now even that would not be enough. After deep discussion, Pat had to agree with her husband. She told Ede that she and George would have to pull Don out of skating for financial reasons.

The news came as a complete surprise and shock to Ede. He begged the Jacksons to reconsider. Don was going to be a world champion, he argued. He offered his services as Don's coach free of charge if the parents would let him continue. His unselfish offer caused Pat and George to change their minds. However, pride, very much a part of their character, would not let the Jacksons take anything free. They stipulated that the coach would have to let them continue paying for his services as best they could. With a great feeling of relief, Ede prepared to work his pupil even harder than before to justify the sacrifice that Pat and George were going to have to make.

Using himself as a model in Goderich, Ede worked on Don's footwork. He had the youngster trail him all over the ice, duplicating each move he made. Much of the half hour in each lesson was spent in these strenuous skating drills in which Don did all he could to keep up with his coach.

Though demanding, Ede did not share Arnold's view that a child must remain silent while working on the ice— especially in the narrow confines of the patch used for figure practice. He felt one reason Don was becoming a great skater was that he was a mischievous boy both on and off the ice. He did not want to make skating a chore

Rehder

Donald—12 years old

Donald—13 years old

Donald and the *Glad Rag Doll*—a comedy number he skated in many carnivals

Don in the Minto Follies (Ottawa)—1954

for his protégé and therefore tolerated many of Don's antics during practice.

Yet, there is a limit to everyone's tolerance level. One day that summer, Don found Ede's breaking point. Ede had taught Don how to perform a double axel jump that Don began to land on one foot finally—but not perfectly—that day. Though not landing precisely as he should, the jumps were being executed in a spectacular manner with Don travelling as much as ten feet in the air and performing his two and a half revolutions at a reduced speed.

When the practice was over, Ede, aware of how hard he had worked Don that day, told him he could go home or stay and practice a few more double axels at the other end of the rink if he wasn't too tired. Meanwhile, Ede had another lesson to teach. Don smiled and immediately sped off towards the other end of the rink apparently eager to practice the double axel he had almost mastered.

A short while later, however, Ede glanced up from his lesson to see Don not practising any jumps but rolling around on the ice like a child in a crib! The coach stopped his lesson, excused himself in as poised a manner as possible, and then sped down the entire length of the rink and smacked Don such a blow on the back of the head that it sent him sprawling.

Tears welled up in Don's eyes, not so much from the pain of the blow as to his embarrassment about letting his coach down. Ede, meanwhile, felt just as badly about hitting his pupil. He immediately skated over to where his parents were sitting and apologized for hitting their son. Though a gentleman, never prone to use even the mildest of expletives, Ede could not restrain himself. He blurted out: "The little rascal was just fooling around over there!"

The lesson was well-taken. Don began to perform better and better as the summer passed. He attempted and passed his Fifth Test and soon began to land a jump that Ede himself had almost landed back in 1950 just before he had come to Canada. Five years before, a triple jump was no more than a mere possibility, yet here was Ede's pupil attempting a triple salchow at thirteen years of age!

It had been a great summer for Don. He was becoming well known in skating circles. More and more people began to talk of him as a potential future great. He headed back home knowing that now, more than ever, plenty of ice time was absolutely essential. Plans were underway to increase ice time for Don at the club during the following fall-winter season. Then, disaster struck. The arena burned down on September 15th. How could he get any ice time at all now, and keep on at school? For a few days it seemed his career in skating had come to at least a temporary halt.

But out of the setback came something new, different, and good for Don. The members banded together and toured towns in the surrounding area. They'd give exhibitions, stage carnivals and do production numbers in order to gain ice time.

The exposure to differing audiences was a great help to Don. That's when he first put together a comedy routine called "Glad Rag Doll" with a life size Raggedy Ann doll that his mother had created for him. The doll faced him, its feet tied to the tops of his skating boots. He skated to the tune *Rag Time Doll*, following the events described in the song's lyrics. Audiences loved it. George, taking a big interest in the shows, became their publicity agent, creating eye-catching posters with his excellent talent in calligraphy.

George also spent a lot of time driving Donald to and

from such towns as Stouffville, Bowmanville and Port Perry for ice time and practice. Others drove Don to other rinks when George wasn't available. Ede, now teaching in Peterborough, would drive to Oshawa on Sundays, picking Don up at seven a.m. so they could be back in Peterborough and on the ice by nine. Don would work hard for the next three hours and then was finished for the day. But Ede wasn't. He'd teach until ten at night. Don spent the afternoons mingling with juniors at the Peterborough club and playing with them at every opportunity. With the two hour ride back, Don would get home at midnight! It never ceased to amaze Ede how eager his pupil was every Sunday morning at seven and how polite he still was at ten in the evening. Such a willingness to sacrifice so much to obtain ice time was one of the characteristics that Ede felt was going to create the world champion he knew Don could be.

Not all of Don's performances were as pleasing for the audience as they had been. Ede had put together a carnival in Peterborough at the time. One pantomime routine had Don playing the role of Peter Pan. Don's skating was excellent, but his acting brought no life to the character of Peter Pan at all, even after much coaxing and coaching. It became apparent to Ede that Don loved to skate and entertain audiences with skating and skating alone, not with acting.

But it was Don's skating that began to worry Ede soon thereafter. The financial strain of commuting was becoming too heavy again for the Jacksons. Ede felt he could no longer help develop Don's skating technique on the kind of ice time made necessary by a commuter's schedule. He

Arnold Gerschwiler, famous world coach from Great Britain, who taught
Donald in the summer of 1952 at Stratford, Ontario, shown here with his pupil
Sjoukje Dijkstra, former World and Olympic Champion

Rehder

Minto Follies—1954. L to R: Carol Heiss, Charles Snelling, Gundi Busch,
Don Jackson, Governor-General Vincent Massey

therefore advised Don and his parents that it was time they looked for another good coach somewhere else who could offer Don the necessary ice time.

A short while later, in March of 1954, the Jacksons received a letter from Arnold Gerschwiler who was teaching in England. He felt Don had the makings of a great skater and wanted him to come to England and aim for the English championship, which is open to Canadians as Commonwealth members.

With financial resources down to almost nothing, the Jacksons borrowed money to buy a one-way boat ticket for their son to travel to England that summer and train under Gerschwiler. Meanwhile Don performed in various carnivals and shows to keep in shape. In May, he journeyed to Ottawa to participate in the Minto club carnival there. That was an important trip for him. His skating greatly impressed Minto club officials and some Canadian Figure Skating Association members who were at the carnival. When they learned of Don's imminent departure to train in England, they sought a way to keep him in Canada.

They found one. A sponsorship programme was set up. Don would get guaranteed ice time at the Minto club along with a place to stay during the winter. Would the Jacksons accept? Again, they were torn. Their financial problems would be taken care of by the proposal. But they still hesitated. They remembered what Arnold had been able to accomplish with their son during that recent summer in Stratford. Arnold, of course, also had Ede's vote as the best of tutors. The decision weighed heavily on Pat and George. They did not want to go against the wishes of the Canadian officials. At the same time, they wanted the best possible training conditions for their son, a main prerequisite of which was a good coach.

The final decision came when the top pro at the Minto club agreed to become Don's full-time coach. Among his coaching achievements had been teaching the beautiful Barbara Ann Scott, whose skating show Don had thrilled to only a few years before. The Jacksons chose Ottawa. But that wouldn't start until autumn. How about the summer? The Minto pro had the answer to that, as well. He would be teaching that summer at Laval, a suburb of Montreal. The Jacksons cashed the ticket to England and thus brought together enough money to finance Don for a summer stay in Montreal with his new coach.

3
Otto

Although his most spectacular success had been in coaching Barbara Ann Scott, Otto Gold also was recognized as a master of teaching school figures to his skaters. He believed strongly in the basic figures as an integral part of higher level figures training and worked Don hard building on the extensive background that Don had acquired in basic figures through his many early test failures. The training technique instituted by Otto paid early dividends. Don passed his Seventh Test during that initial training season at Laval. Passing the test made Don eligible for the Canadian Junior Men's championships. That event was his goal when he arrived in Ottawa in the fall.

Having observed his new pupil intently over the summer, Otto felt Don's skating needed a lot of work to raise it to the level needed for a competition milieu. He thought the music in Don's free skating programme stayed too far in the background. The programme itself was a dazzling array of jumps, accompanied by a few spins and some footwork. Don had practised hard on his footwork with Ede. But Otto felt it was not good enough to be competitive nationally or internationally.

Accordingly, Otto set out to direct Don's skating straight at the needs of competition. With his great body control, learned under Ede, Don quickly implemented the school

Otto Gold and Don (1956)

figures, which Otto wished to make part of his footwork. As the winter passed on, he became more and more adept at skating a solid routine to music while at the same time perfecting his figures.

The Canadian Championships were in the third week in January, 1955, bringing Don his first chance to compete at the national level. He almost missed that chance due to his love of comedy routines. A few weeks before the competition, he fell badly during a comedy routine in a show, receiving a concussion and a badly gashed forehead. But the game little youth was not about to let a fall keep him from his first big competition. The next day he returned to the ice as if nothing had happened.

Because of family finances, Don was still using $12.50 skating boots. To one pair were attached the blades used for figures; the other pair was used for free skating. When Ede had told him that a skater with good body control could skate well on any quality of boot, Don had believed him. But the day before the championships he started to have doubts. He stepped onto the ice to practise his figures. One circle felt fine. The other felt alarmingly odd. He stopped and tried to dull one of his blades but found no improvement. What a time for his skates to fall apart on him! Noticing the concern on Don's normally happy face, Otto called him over and asked him what was wrong. Don told him. Otto then calmly said, "Check the boots". Don did. To his surprise, he found that in his haste to get on the ice, he had put on one boot for figures and one for free skating. Later, with the proper boots on, he worked twice as long on his figures as on his free skating. The move paid off. The next day, to everyone's astonishment except Otto's, Don

Members of the Minto Skating Club, Ottawa, who competed in the 1955 Canadian Championships. Standing, L to R: Don Jackson, Frances Gold; seated, at rear: Nancy Davidson, Heather West, Claire Nettleton, Carol Jane Pachl

Dinsmore

Don on practice patch for the 1955 Junior Canadian Championships—warming up for the backward outside loops

won the figures part of the Junior Men's competition. Bob Paul, second, had been considered a shoo-in to win. Pat and George were in a state of ecstasy. Otto was pleased—but managed to keep it under control. He sent Don right back to the ice after everyone else had left, to practise his figures some more.

All that remained was for Don to go out and skate the way he and everyone else knew he could in the free skating programme. If he did, he'd win. The next day, about a half hour before he was due to perform, Don walked casually into the dressing room to begin changing into his skating uniform. Laughing and kidding with his dad as he laid out his gear, Don suddenly went pale. He looked frantically around. He couldn't find his pants!

At first George thought his son was kidding around as usual. But this was too good to be acting. Then they remembered. Don's pants had been sent to the hotel cleaners. In their rush to leave for the arena, neither had noticed that the pants hadn't been returned. George made a dash for the hotel to try and retrieve the pants in time.

Most skaters from the Minto club had money. As a result, Otto had booked the entire club team into the Royal York Hotel, Toronto's most exclusive hotel at the time. But it was too rich for the Jacksons. When Don brought news of the booking home to his parents, they'd told Don that he would have to stay with them in the much less expensive Ford Hotel.

The change in hotels was a stroke of luck now. The Royal York was away downtown in Toronto, the Ford much closer. George ran, had some agonizing trouble getting out of the jammed parking lot, made it, raced for the hotel and ran up the stairs to the room. The pants were neatly hung on the back of the door. He grabbed them and got back to the arena less than five minutes before his son was due to go on.

Did the crisis bother Don? Not that anyone could notice. He skated a programme that brought one of the greatest ovations ever heard at Varsity Arena. With a performance like that, there was nothing Bob Paul could do to win. Don had won the national Junior Men's title the very first time out. Now offers for show performances from all over Ontario began to pour in. Otto, recalling Don's concussion a few weeks before, flatly forbade Don to accept any offers to perform comedy routines. He did say that any show that requested Don to perform only his competition solo was acceptable as far as he was concerned. The decision to accept would still be Don's.

Meanwhile, recognition of Don's achievement came from circles outside of skating as well. Immediately upon his return to Ottawa, Don was awarded that city's crest in honour of his victory. Later, when spring arrived, the city again honoured the young skater by giving him the city's official commemorative gold medal. So he was getting lots of glory. But as with all amateurs, glory is not something one can put in the bank. Although the Ottawa family Don stayed with that winter had not asked payment from the Jacksons, there had been expense in Don's schooling. Pat and George also as usual insisted on paying what they could for board. This was still well below the normal. With another summer of skating expenses around the corner, financial strain again threatened the Jackson household. Once more help arrived from concerned people in the skating world. An Ottawa family, the Dillinghams, offered to sponsor Don. They agreed that the Jacksons would pay what they could, but set up the sponsorship to meet expenses above what the Jacksons could afford—this being the total

amount of Pat's salary, as it had been now for years.

With finances thus settled once again, Don was able to accompany Otto and his daughter to Lake Placid, New York, to train for the summer. Also, at Otto's suggestion, Don purchased his first pair of custom-made boots. With many skaters training at Lake Placid, a show was inevitable. Don was asked to skate his solo routine. Unaccustomed to skating in a spotlight, he soon began to consider it a great performance if he fell only once during his programme. The spotlight men apparently sensed his uneasiness and began to place bets among themselves as to how many times he would fall in a given show and how many times they could cause him to fall by turning off the houselights and making him skate solely in the spotlight.

Don was living with Otto and his daughter and a few other Canadians in one house which quickly became labelled "Canada House" by the American skaters staying nearby. Good-natured prank playing was commonplace with Don at the centre of everything. One of his achievements in retaliation for an American gag, was to sneak into one of the "America Houses" and lay leftover chicken legs in all the beds.

Mischievous though he was, Don was also growing up. He began to notice girls, and one in particular, from South Carolina. He struggled inwardly for the courage to hold her hand. Two weeks before he was due to return to Canada, a party was being given for some skaters. Don was invited to attend. The girl from South Carolina would also be there. Offered a golden opportunity, Don declined. He explained that he was returning to Canada to attempt his Eighth and final figures test and didn't want to jeopardize his chances

Don Jackson and Wanda Beasley—Junior Canadian Singles Champions—1955

by upsetting his normal routine. The truth was a little different. He was really afraid of having to deal with girls in public. All the same, nobody would ever know. Back in Canada two weeks later, he passed the test on the first try. With that highest level test now under his belt, he was eligible for the top rung of national competition: the Senior Men's championships. This meant, among other things, moving up his free skating programme to five minutes. He'd needed only four to win the junior meet in January.

Back at the Minto Club in early autumn, Otto noticed that Don had begun to mature physically. Otto became even more demanding. Though Don was by far the fastest skater around, and could attain unbelievable height and distance from his jumps, Otto wanted him to skate faster and jump higher and higher than ever before, now that he was stronger. His coach never let up. Many times Don would be frustrated. After practising axel after axel and reaching what he thought was the best height and distance ever, he would skate back to his coach expecting at least a little praise. Otto would frown slightly and say, "Why don't you stop doing those bunny hops and start jumping?"

Otto had other gimmicks intended to better his skaters' performances. One all the skaters liked. Worried above all about the school figures, Otto would have each national skater he coached (Eddie Collins, Don, his daughter Frances, Carol Jane Pachl and Dick Rimmer) perform the figures in turn, with the others acting as judges. Once in awhile, Otto would bring in official judges to add a measure of realism. And, to add even more difficulty and excitement to the contest, he would sometimes turn off all the arena lights so they'd have to perform their figures in semi-darkness.

Otto hoped that the little intra-group contests might give his skaters more confidence in their figures. He needed no help, however, in Don's case where free skating was concerned. Don had made known early his ambition to become the world's best free skater. But for Otto that was not enough. The best free skater in the world stands little chance of winning a major competition if he does not also feel in his heart that he can beat anybody at figures too.

This of course involves a lot of practice from which good figures can be produced, which then give the skater confidence in his own ability. Accordingly, Otto was understandably upset one day when he arrived late for practise (but earlier than he had said he would arrive) and found the rink and his skaters in a state of chaos.

The skaters had been told to practise their basic figures on their respective patches before their coach's arrival. They'd started out to do just that. However, Don wanted to have a little fun. He went over to a friend's patch and put a skid mark right through it rendering the patch useless for figure practise. The friend returned the favour. Then she and Don picked on another. Before long, all patches had been skidded over, and the five seniors were having a free-for-all skating party on the ice when their coach walked in. Several hours and many miles of figures later, the five decided they had better concentrate on skating the next time they were left alone to do so.

One day in practise Don added a unique step to his already fancy footwork. Trying to do a regular slow turn with the rotating foot in the back, he caught his skating blade in a rut in the ice and began to fall forward. In an effort to regain his balance, he swiftly brought the rotating leg forward and found to his surprise that it not only

steadied his balance, but felt good. He tried the move that way a few more times before showing it to some of the other seniors. They laughed, but their laughter quickly abated when Otto watched the move and became very enthused with it. He told Don to practise it more so that they could incorporate it into his programme.

Shortly thereafter, Don went to Galt to compete in his initial Senior Men's nationals. Skating well, he managed a strong second place finish behind Charles Snelling. Experience seemed to be the main quality lacking in his performances—a factor that only time could ameliorate.

Don again spent the summer in Lake Placid with Otto and his daughter and worked hard. He was preparing himself for his biggest competitive winter season yet—the possibility of skating in three major meets—the Canadian Senior Men's, North American, and World Championships. At the end of the summer, he returned home to Oshawa for a rare stay that lasted over a month.

While at home, he spent some time keeping himself in shape so that he could resume heavy training immediately upon his return to Ottawa. He found his dad much more understanding and knowledgeable about his sport now. This brought Don extra pleasure. In an effort to grasp what was going on in the sport his son seemed so intent upon mastering, George was working hard to help other Oshawa club members, driving skaters to and from practices and competitions in other cities. He was president for two years of the Interclub competitions that Ede had founded. Pat was also very pleased and relieved at George's involvement. Her husband viewed skating from a different perspective

Van

Donald with his $12.50 boots he wore when he won the Canadian Junior Men's title

Don's first year in Senior Canadian Championships—Galt, 1956. A good-luck kiss from Linda Ward, who became Canadian Junior Pairs Champion in 1963 with Neil Carpenter

Mayor Charlotte Whitton of Ottawa presents the crest of the City to 1955 Canadian Champions Don Jackson, Junior Men, and Carol Jane Pachl, Senior Ladies, while their coach Otto Gold looks on

now. Financial arguments of the past had faded to zero.

Don's first major competition of the season was the North American championships in Rochester, for once held ahead of the Canadian Senior Men's event. He trained hard again during the fall. On the first day of competition, he went out and won the first figure. Not only was he surprised, but David Jenkins of the U.S., who eventually won the gold medal, scratched his head and, somewhat startled, wondered out loud about who the little squirt was from Canada who had just walked in there and come out on top after the first figure.

With only six skaters in the competition, Don had to return to the ice to practise for his next figure before Otto had a chance to tell him he'd won the first figure. That information might have helped. Anyway, Don blew his next three figures, falling far down from the top position he had occupied at the outset. But Don's troubles were not over.

When Don had returned to Ottawa in the fall, he and Otto had decided to put together a completely new free skating programme. They had only a couple of months to prepare it for competition. Don skated well during the early stages of the five minute routine but took a fall at the half way mark. He was back on his feet in a flash continuing his performance. Yet, his desire was not enough to overcome his inexperience with the programme. He fell three times in the final minute. This eliminated him from the medals. He finished fourth.

His parents consoled him by saying that fourth place was a respectable finish for the youngest competitor who had, on top of that handicap, skated a programme with which he was unfamiliar. But the placing meant little to Don. He was concerned mainly with the fact that he had fallen four times in the last half of his free skating. That was supposed to be his strength. He wanted to become the best free-skater in the world. He resolved to himself to have the situation settled by the middle of February when he would be in Winnipeg competing in the Canadian Senior Men's Championships.

He was much better in Winnipeg, but could not improve upon his second place of the year before. Still, he finished closer to Charles Snelling this time and did not fall during his free skating programme. Also, a second place finish meant that Don was eligible to represent Canada at the World Championships in Colorado Springs two weeks later. Should he go? Otto said okay, if he wanted. The international experience would be good. But there were hitches to be worked out. First, there was the two-week delay. Otto felt it would be a waste of time and money to return to Ottawa from Winnipeg, only to fly back west later to Colorado. Then came a stroke of luck. The Fort William Skating Club asked Don to perform in their carnival. In return, they offered to look after his fare from Fort William to Colorado Springs and then back to Ottawa. Don quickly accepted the generous offer after the club also met Otto's conditions—that Don receive adequate ice time for practice.

In the excitement about his prospects for the World's, Don had one disappointment. Otto would not make the trip with him to Colorado Springs. If he did, the Jacksons would be paying his fare and Otto thought it was too much money to spend on a competition in which Don was participating for experience and exposure only. He also felt that Don needed the opportunity to stand on his own two feet at major competitions and deal on his own with the increased pressure that inevitably accompanies the biggest meet in the world. Otto told his pupil he had confidence in his

ability, but not to expect too much; he'd do well to finish in the top ten, maybe as high as seventh—if he skated very well.

Don headed off to Fort William. He worked as well as he could on his own with his figures. At night he got good experience skating his solo for the carnival audiences. At the end of the two weeks, he was confident and eager to be on his way.

He arrived in Colorado Springs alone, a little more apprehensive now about dealing with a strange environment on his own. He was delighted to find Dick McLaughlin of Oshawa at the competition as a judge. Through George's involvement in the Oshawa skating club after Don's departure, Dick had become a close friend of the family. He kept an eye on Don before the competition.

While practising his jumps one day, Don was also happy to see his old part-time coach, Arnold Gerschwiler. Arnold had come to the championships only to observe—or so Don thought at first. That day Arnold asked him to continue jumping and commented on how he was doing. After several jumps Don would stop and start to skate off the ice. Arnold would ask to see just a few more jumps. Don, naïve to say the least, was happy for the help he thought he was getting.

Meanwhile, another Canadian coach had been observing Don. After fifteen or twenty minutes, he came to Don and said that it might be a good idea to stop for the day, go home, rest up for the competition. Arnold smiled weakly and quickly nodded approval before thanking Don and excusing himself. When they were alone, the coach, Sheldon

Harry Josephson

Marg and Bruce Hyland

Don Jackson and Wendy Griner practicing for their dance tests at Weston, where they were coached by Marg and Bruce Hyland. Don and Wendy were Senior Canadian Champions together in 1960, 1961 and 1962

Harry Josephson

Don shown with some of his trophies and a plaque with the "Key to the City" presented to him by Fort William, Ontario, now part of Thunder Bay

Galbraith (who later would play a significant role in Don's life) mentioned to Don that Arnold had come over with a skater from England who was at about the same level as Don. He should be aware of that situation. Don protested in Arnold's defence at the time but was a little less sure of that protest later when he finished just one place ahead of Arnold's pupil.

Though he was again the youngest competitor, Don did not let that drawback affect his confidence. He skated to a very respectable tenth place finish in the figures part of the competition. He then came back the next day and glided through an excellent free skating programme which earned him fifth spot in that category and moved him up to seventh place over-all, the finish that Otto told him he could hope for with a very good performance.

The placing was an excellent one for a sixteen-year-old boy in his first world championship. Everyone who knew the Jacksons deluged them with congratulatory mail. Don was also happy with what he had done. But he knew the experience had been the most valuable part. It opened his eyes to many things, including politics in sports.

One thing he subsequently pondered was his position at the Minto Club. For several months prior to the World's, Otto had been asking him to demonstrate various facets of skating to his daughter and the other members of the club from time to time. Honoured at the invitation, he had been more than happy to do the demonstrations. Yet, upon his return from Colorado Springs, he found that the demands were now daily ones. He questioned what kind of progress he could hope to make when he was spending most of his practice time demonstrating for others.

Otto's daughter had reached the stage where she was ready to make it into the top levels of competition. By realising that it was only natural for a parent to want the best for his or her child, Don was able to take an understanding view of the near total commitment Otto was now showing towards his daughter's progress. However, he also realised that he had to worry about his own career. His conclusion was that the time had come to look for another coach.

Only weeks after his return from the World's, he wrote to his parents. He would like, he said, to change coaches. There were other factors as well. Pat and George were a little annoyed that Otto had not stuck to the money-limit agreed upon for Don's lessons. They wrote back to Don giving him the go-ahead. Don left the Minto Club immediately thereafter.

The decision by the Jacksons was a big one. Once again, it involved financial sacrifice. The sponsorships Don had received were contingent on Don being in Ottawa. George was now making sixty dollars per week and Pat forty-five. Without crippling the family in other areas, they simply didn't have enough to pay for Don's full time participation in skating. And it would get worse. His higher level of competition meant soaring increases in travel expenses. On top of that, they had to worry about debts they had built up in Ottawa.

Nevertheless, they set their financial worries aside for the moment and concentrated on helping Don find a new coach. After much thought, the family decided that the decision would be made between Gus Lussi, who had been coaching at Lake Placid at the same time that Don had been there training with Otto, and Pierre Brunet who was coaching in New York City.

The choice was difficult. Lussi was well known for his expertise in jumping and spinning. Don had at least seen

him while at Lake Placid. Brunet, on the other hand, was known for his success in coaching Carol Heiss who had won the women's world singles title for the past two years. The choice was finally made when Dick McLaughlin was asked by the Jacksons to express his opinion as a long time friend, skating expert, administrator and judge.

Bob McIntyre

Pierre Brunet and Don

A fantastic group of Pierre Brunet's pupils at the Skating Club of New York upstairs in the old Madison Square Garden. L to R: Nancy Heiss, Carol Heiss, Carol Wanek, Don Jackson, Alain Giletti, Alain Calmat, four of whom won World titles

4

Pierre

Pat and Don stared disbelievingly at the sign over the flea-bag hotel to which they had just been directed.

"This can't be the right place," Pat said, shocked at what was to be her son's home for the next year.

Don replied, "I know this is it. Mr. Brunet said that the Belvedere was right across the street from the rink. It must look better inside. He did say that he had stayed here and that it was very nice, didn't he?"

"It may very well have been when he stayed here, but that was fifteen years ago and I don't think the place has improved any with age," mused Pat. "However, we've no alternative. You might as well learn to like it. Besides, Mr. Brunet does seem to know what he is doing. . . ."

That was an oblique reference to the summer—and what a summer it had been. The decision to go with Pierre Brunet had been largely based on the excellent figures that Carol Heiss and all Pierre's skaters had shown in competition. When Don had arrived at Pierre's summer skating school in East Lansing, Michigan, he had brought with him determination, dedication, motivation. What had impressed Pierre along with these qualities was that, even at 17, Don seemed to know that success came only through hard work. It remained only for the coach to set the right course.

Pierre carefully mapped out the programme he believed could send Don to the top of the skating world.

The fine jumping base that had been laid by Ede and enlarged by Otto brought Don to the stage where he felt he was capable of attempting the first-ever triple lutz jump. With unbounded enthusiasm he had begun to work on the jump with Pierre. It became an obsession. When success had appeared to be close, he redoubled his concentration and efforts—and then Pierre slowed him down, on purpose. He felt that somehow he had to get Don away from the historic jump and back to improving his general skating technique. Pierre was sure then that Don would become the first person ever to perform a triple lutz successfully in competition, but the rest of his free skating programme was not up to those standards. He impressed upon Don that it was necessary to build a programme that would keep the judges interested throughout the entire five minutes. A triple lutz would be a spectacular achievement, but it would take only a few seconds. What then? If there was nothing around it of near-equal value, Don might not receive proper credit for completing this near-impossible jump. But how does one tell a starry-eyed hard-working seventeen-year-old that he has to work on other things than making history? Fortunately for Pierre (and, eventually, Don) fate had lent a hand.

One day, working hard on the triple lutz, Don fell and severely sprained his ankle. Pierre seized the opportunity. He asked the doctor to put Don into a walking foot cast for a couple of weeks. Don could skate with a sprained ankle. But even he wouldn't be likely to try a triple lutz in a cast.

Don, unaware of the real reason behind the cast, accepted it as part of the hazards of his sport. But that was not enough for Pierre. To keep Don's mind completely off skating, he sent Don to his cottage to relax. Relax? Don spent the two weeks cleaning stones and pebbles off the

beach that was part of the cottage property; one hundred wheel-barrow loads did it nicely.

When the cast was removed, Don had just one week to prepare for his eighth level (gold) American test. What surprised him most was that having been off skates for a couple of weeks, his figures, instead of deteriorating, had greatly improved. When he finished the figure portion of the test, one judge remarked that it was the best test she had ever judged.

It was not so, however, with the free skating portion of the test. The layoff had hurt Don's conditioning there. To add to his problem, his music was played too quickly. By the time the five minutes had ended, Don had barely enough energy to skate off the ice. However, the performance was good enough to grab a passing grade even though he'd been chasing all over the ice to catch up to his music and perform his jumps on time. Don's music that day was from the opera *Carmen*, music that would take on great significance for him several years later.

Anyway, summer was over. So was a brief visit home that had turned out extremely well in more ways than one.

Even though he had just finished a season of skating, Don had not been able to stay away from the few rinks in Toronto that were operating as Fall schools. At one rink he was asked if he would mind skating with a young girl named Barbara Beatty, to help her pass one of the dance tests she was working on. Don said sure. Barbara passed her test. Her father, Tim Beatty, was impressed with the manner in which Don had unselfishly aided his daughter. He got together with a friend of his, Percy Law. They decided to sponsor Don to make up for what he had lost by leaving Ottawa.

This help enabled Pat to accompany Don and help him get settled in his new home. She was again silently thanking her son's benefactors as she led him into the shabby building and up to the front desk of the hotel.

Don's room turned out to be no better than the outside of the hotel. It was simple, sparsely furnished. A small refrigerator and hot plate were inside a closet. This would be the source of Don's "home cooked" meals. A musty smell permeated the place. A dirty, tattered rug covered the floor. A number of cockroaches flitted about. However, Don was not going to complain. He was happy to be in New York. Pierre had chosen this place for its proximity to the rink and to keep costs down. He'd come this far, and across the street at Madison Square Garden a vital new phase of his career was about to begin. Who cared about a room?

When Don showed up for his first lesson he found that Pierre had arranged for two French skaters, Alain Giletti and Alain Calmat, to take rooms in the Belvedere as well. The company would make living there more bearable for them all. Pierre also outlined to Don the two aspects of his skating they were going to concentrate on: first, school figures and how they could be applied to his free skating programme; second, consistency in jumping.

In the latter area, Pierre, like so many others who had watched Don on his jumps, could only be astonished at the over-all picture of grandeur they presented. There was the speed of take-off, the great height attained, the distance travelled. The devil-may-care attitude that Don projected also made his jumps appear even more spectacular. Yet there remained a degree of inconsistency that had to be eliminated if Don was to reach the heights.

There were times when Don, at the top of a jump, appeared to lean at an almost impossible 45° angle. With almost any other skater this always would have meant a bad fall. Don would right himself at the last instant and land on one foot. His unbelievable reflexes almost always saved him. Very few athletes possessed his qualities to such a degree. Pierre realized that if he could harness these natural resources to provide a greater degree of consistency, Don Jackson would become the ultimate skater and competitor.

Pierre's decision was to have Don go back to the very basics of jumping, starting with constant work on the loop jump. His reasoning was that in the loop the landing foot was always the one used on the take-off. If Don's balance was poor on take-off, it would cause the landing to be less controlled or missed completely. The remedy was to be consistently good on take-off. Don found himself doing more single (and later double) loop jumps in a week than he had done in a month with his previous coaches. The theory Pierre expounded appeared sound. Don's jumping showed a marked improvement in consistency as time went on.

Yet, consistency in one area alone was not the only thing Pierre had in mind when he began drilling Don on the loop jumps. The astute coach realised that increased consistency would lead directly to increased confidence, with both consistency and confidence spreading to the execution of all Don's jumps. Pierre wanted this confidence to pervade Don's entire programme and make it all flow with equal ease. All this Pierre felt was the important step in creating a programme that would not suffer in comparison to the majestic quality of a first ever triple lutz jump.

On the way to Paris and the 1958 World Championships.
L to R: Nancy Heiss, Carol Heiss, Don Jackson, Carol
Wanek, Pierre Brunet

Toronto Telegram

Taken during the winning performance at
the 1959 Canadian Championships at Varsity Arena in Toronto

Powell Photo Studi

The Minto Cup for 1959 Canadian Senior
Men's Championship being presented to Don
by Mr. E. R. S. (Dick) McLaughlin, President of the Canadian Figure Skating Association.

The months passed. Don, sensing his improvement, began to develop an insatiable appetite for workouts—at the expense of his nutritional appetite. Not especially savoring one of his own closet-cooked meals, Don started to skip lunches and stayed at the rink to skate on his own—a situation that appeased his workout appetite and helped him forget about his nutritional one. A young body can withstand for a short time the stress placed upon it through exertion without sufficient nutrition. But not even Don's tremendous desire could have kept his body functioning at that pace for long. He might have been headed for another illness, due to malnutrition. But near Christmas in 1957, he got an unexpected break.

Pierre, always wanting his skaters to perform as often as possible in front of audiences, accepted an invitation for Don to skate in a New York ice show. Don with his new-found confidence and style, eagerly looked forward to the night. As he skated his routine, his broad smile along with his superb skating quickly brought the crowd to his side as it had done so many times before. Particularly impressed were a New York couple named Coryn. As they watched his flashing smile speeding about the ice surface, the Coryns decided to take an active interest in Don's career. They enquired. They found out where he was living. They found that he was skipping meals. So, they immediately wrote to Pat and asked if Don could board with them. Finances and Don's meals made for a quick decision. The Jacksons said yes.

Another break was that it gave Don a family Christmas. His parents could not afford to pay his fare home. Still wanting to see him, Pat and George found out that a special

1959 North American Champions. L to R: Robert Paul, Barbara Wagner, Carol Heiss, Donald Jackson, Geraldine Fenton, William McLachlan

Preparing for the World's—Pierre Brunet and his pupils: Don, and Nancy and Carol Heiss

64

Christmas show to be filmed in front of a large New York City department store would include a segment devoted to passersby on the street. They told Don. He went to the store at the designated time and gradually worked his way up to the front and waved frantically into the camera, holding a sign that read "Merry Christmas, Mom, Dad and Bill". In Oshawa, Pat and George intently watched their TV set in an effort to spot their son, but without success. Though Don's timing on his jumps was improving, his timing for TV was a little off. He had waved into the camera while a commercial was being shown.

Even though his parents had failed to see him on TV, it was only a matter of weeks before they did see him in person. The Canadian Senior Championships were in Ottawa. For the third successive year, he finished second to Charles Snelling. Again he had qualified to represent Canada at the World Championships, this time, 1958, to be held in Paris.

Excitement and nervous tension took over when Don arrived in Paris for the competition. Pierre stressed that this was to be his first exposure in Europe and that it was very important that he make a good first impression on judges and various other officials. His start was none too auspicious: ninth in the figures, an improvement of one place over the previous year. Disappointed but definitely not through, Don prepared himself for the free skating, to be held the next day. With his new-found confidence and consistency, thanks to the many hours of loops and double loops Pierre had put him through, he skated a magnificent programme to pull his final standing up to fourth place. When the scores were separated and analyzed, Don learned

Donald Jackson

George Gross and Pat Jackson at the Broadmoor pool
discussing Don's chances in the 1959 World's

Bob McIntyre

Medal winners at the 1959 World's. L to R: David Jenkins—Gold;
Donald Jackson—Silver; Tim Brown—Bronze

he had ranked in free skating second only to the winner David Jenkins, who remembered him well as the little guy from Canada who had won the first figure at the North American championships the year before.

Don's first impression on the European skating community was indeed a good one. He received invitations to skate exhibitions in several European cities immediately following the World championships. Though happy with his pupil's successes, Pierre already was thinking ahead. In the Summer programme, he was going to have to help Don improve his figures still further to complement his great free skating abilities. Only in that combination could he cross the final bridge to world supremacy.

As the Summer training began, Pierre redoubled his efforts. He drilled Don on the importance of full body control: knowing exactly what he was doing and why every second he was on the ice. A perfectionist, Pierre worked his pupil constantly to the goal of being able to do a figure without forcing the edge. He would not be pleased until a figure had been executed with absolutely no snow on the edge of the print on the ice. Sometimes he would spend an hour and a half with Don on just the changing of an edge. But even an enthusiastic youngster can become bored with such a routine. Don did. One day Pierre took Don aside to explain once again the importance of the tedious work Don was doing.

"Imagine yourself in a restaurant, Don. The waiter goes by with a tray of plates and bumps into another waiter. The accident causes a plate to fly off the tray. The waiter makes a great catch with his free hand to save the plate from

A spectacular array of skating talent on the European Tour after the 1959 World's, at Templehof Airport, West Berlin. L to R: Alain Giletti, Marika Kilius, Hans-Jürgen Bäumler, Ina Bauer, Jean Paul Guhel, Anna Galmarini, Sjoukje Dijkstra, Donald Jackson, Nancy Heiss, Karol Divin, Barbara Wagner, Carol Heiss, Alain Calmat, Bob Paul

breaking. Now what would you say about the waiter's ability?"

"I'd say he's pretty good!" Don said.

"OK, but suppose the same thing happens five more times and each time the waiter misses the falling plate and it breaks. What would your opinion be?"

"That he was lucky the first time and really didn't know what he was doing," answered Don.

"Exactly!" stressed Pierre. "He didn't know what he was doing. In other words, he didn't have full control of his body movements or else he would have been able to catch the plate every time. Well, it's the same with your figures, Don. They are going to teach you to know your body so that every time you formulate a movement on the ice, be it a figure, jump, or spin, you will be able to do it consistently well because you will have full control over your body during the motion."

The lesson ended on that note. Its effects were to be there for a long time. Not once did Don show signs of complaint during the remainder of the Summer and the following Fall skating season. It was this continuing dedication to hard work which was to bring him his first national and international skating victories in the winter of 1959.

Just before he left to compete in the Canadian Senior Championships in Noranda, Quebec in January of '59, Don received an unexpected honour. He was named the King of Winter at the annual Lake Placid winter carnival. He shared the throne with team mate Carol Heiss, who was Queen. Following this, maybe inspired by his new title, Don went to Noranda and proceeded to win his first Canadian senior title.

Gehri

Davos—on tour. L to R: Guy Revell, Debbie Wilkes, Don, Maria and Otto Jelinek

Gehri

Don at Davos—1959

PIERRE

A month later, Don returned to Toronto, where he had won his first Canadian Championship (Junior Men's). In the same Varsity Arena he won his first North American title. The poise that Pierre had been working on paid off. Don skated strongly and confidently on his figures and free skating programme. The knowledge he had gained on the control of his body enabled him to perform one particular jump successfully just as it appeared headed for disaster. This happened in the middle of his programme. Don made his approach for a double axel jump. He was slightly off balance on the take-off. As he took off he fought to regain balance. This took away precious air time. He managed to pull the jump in just before landing, giving the impression of a well executed delayed double axel—a jump not being done with any regularity because of its difficulties. After the competition, some judges approached Don and said they loved his delayed double axel. With Pierre's training in confidence to aid him, he didn't enlighten them, thanking them graciously. Unintentional or not, without his exceptional drilling in body control he never would have made that delayed double axel out of his try at a regular one.

Though the win had been a great one, as he had beaten Tim Brown who had been one place ahead of him at the World's the year before, Don realized that his big test would be at the World's in Colorado Springs at the beginning of March. David Jenkins, World champion, had not been able to attend the North American events due to medical school commitments. But he'd be in Colorado, strong as ever.

Unlike his previous trip to Colorado Springs two years earlier for the World championships, Don this time was accompanied by his personal coach. Pierre's presence

King and Queen of Winter at Lake Placid, Christmas 1959. Stan Benham, World and Olympic bobsled champion, Carol Heiss, Don Jackson

1960 Canadian Senior Champions—Barbara Wagner and Robert Paul, Pairs; Virginia Thompson and William McLachlan, Dance; Wendy Griner, Ladies; Donald Jackson, Men

proved itself significantly in many ways, even before the competition began. Coaches are known to vie with each other, trying to gain an advantage or retain an advantage for their skaters, regardless of how slight. The day before the competition was to start, Don was out on his patch practising his figures when Arnold Gerschwiler arrived on the scene, exchanged pleasantries all around and then suggested that the skaters all move down a patch. The move would have put Don on the end patch, a very disadvantageous place to practise figures. Don had just about agreed to the move when Pierre came up and told Arnold that Don was not moving under any circumstances. At this point, Arnold quietly excused himself in much the same manner he had done two years before. He'd tried, anyway. It was another lesson for Don—but this time in psychology.

In the ensuing days Don skated superbly and brought home a silver medal for Canada in the Men's Singles competition. The winner was David Jenkins—the last man standing between Don and the World title which Ede had envisioned for Don years earlier in Oshawa.

Pierre also was more convinced than ever that Don could be world champion. He set to work to give his student the final aspect of his skating education. The summer months that followed Don's second-place finish in Colorado had great value for Don. Pierre, a philosopher and gentleman, already had done much to gain Don's lasting respect. But he had more to give. All too often a coach will concentrate on the perfection of his skater's abilities on the ice—both mental and physical—and overlook what happens outside the rink. Pierre had definite ideas as to what it took to become a skating champion. One was that it was not

Canadian Olympic Figure Skating Team at Squaw Valley, 1960. L to R: Sheldon Galbraith, team coach, Barbara Wagner, Robert Paul, Wendy Griner, Granville Mayall, President CFSA, Maria Jelinek, Otto Jelinek, Sandra Tewkesbury, Donald Jackson, Donald McPherson

Don and his mother on the way to Europe for the Exhibition Tour after the 1960 Olympics and World's

sufficient to be a champion on the ice only—he had to be a champion off the ice as well. His view was: Skating is a sport of communication in which there are no words. The performance comes from within. If you apply yourself to communicating off the ice, it is that much easier to do so from the ice, as well. According to Pierre, a champion arrives only when he can do everything; much as a musician cannot call himself a master until he is able to play any kind of music in any city's symphony—a status that involves great technical ability as well as the ability to combine with others. Pierre felt after the summer that Don was indeed on this track. He had seen the signs.

In February, 1960, Don went to Regina and won the Canadian Senior Men's title for the second successive year. This qualified him to represent Canada at the Olympics in Squaw Valley that same month. But the Olympics brought a conflict, minor but meaningful, that he had not foreseen.

With a widely acclaimed free skating performance, at the Olympics, Don again pulled himself up from a mediocre showing in the figures. He won the bronze medal. However, the medal win was tainted with a slight degree of disappointment. Although a member of Canada's team, and under the jurisdiction of Canada's team coach, Don had still looked for Pierre's help as his personal coach in getting ready for the competition. But Pierre's star pupil, Carol Heiss, was a heavy favourite to win the Olympic gold medal for the U.S. in the women's singles. It was to her that Pierre had to devote most of his time.

As a result, Don received much of his preparatory help from Canadian team coach Sheldon Galbraith. He'd been the one to aid Don when he was coachless at his first World

To Don Jackson
I thought your skating was wonderful!
Sonja Henie

Sonja Henie

Championship three years before. Every morning Don would show up for practice. Galbraith would be there along with his own star pupil, Wendy Griner. The coach would then flip a coin to see who would have to take the first lesson which was generally a poorer one as the skaters had not yet had time to warm up. This show of fairness greatly impressed Don, especially as it involved the coach's own student.

Thankful for the help and patiently awaiting the outcome of the women's event, Don looked forward to the attention he thought he would get once Carol had won the gold medal. However, when she did, and he pushed off to do his first figure of the men's competition, he looked hopefully to the stands. He could not see Pierre. Though his coach may have been there watching him, Don still felt quite disappointed that he had not made himself available after Carol's victory.

A week after the conclusion of the Olympics, Don went to compete for the World Championship in Vancouver. He placed second by a mere tenth of a point behind Alain Giletti although he handily won the free skating portion of the competition. In analyzing his loss Don blamed himself. He believed that his mistake was in starting to pay attention to the glowing praise heaped on him by the press and public. This has proven to be the downfall of many an athlete. Don had now begun to compete against the other competitors. Up to then he had competed mainly with himself: if he was satisfied with his performance, and if in his mind he had improved over the previous time, he was happy. In following this belief he knew that eventually he would reach the goal of near perfection that he had set

1961 Canadian Senior Champions—Wendy Griner, Ladies; Donald Jackson, Men; Otto and Maria Jelinek, Pairs; Virginia Thompson and Wlliam Mc-Lachlan, Dance

Bradley Lord and Donald Jackson, US and Canadian Senior Champions, during practice for the 1961 North Americans at Philadelphia Skating Club and Humane Society

himself. Time in the not too distant future would prove him right.

The time had come once again for Don to face finances. Though Pat and George were receiving help, recent travel expenses had drained them financially. George once again questioned the family's ability to support such a costly endeavour. Don pleaded with them to let him continue until he could become world champion. Tim Beatty, his sponsor, was so impressed with Don's determination that he argued strongly to give him another chance. Once again Pat and George said go ahead. The scare propelled Don to tax himself even harder in workouts.

On January 27th, 1961, Don put on another great free skating performance in Montreal to capture his third consecutive Canadian Senior Men's title. After his performance, Don skated to the side of the rink to await his marks from the judges. When the announcer asked for the marks based on the technical merit of the programme, Don looked over and saw the most beautiful sight he had ever seen—a 6.0! He had received his first *perfect* mark! Inspired by the result, he travelled to Philadelphia a few weeks later and won the North American title for the second time in a row.

After his win in Philadelphia, Don made the short trip back to New York to begin his final preparation with Pierre for the World Championships scheduled for Prague the next month. Because he was already in New York and could not afford a return flight home at the time, Don and his parents informed the Canadian Figure Skating Association that he would fly to the competition with the U.S. team, leaving from New York. The fact that eventually he did not, saved his life.

Don had skated the North Americans with a temperature of 103. Upon his return to New York, his doctor sent him to bed and told him he'd have to book passage to Prague later. While in bed, Don received news of one of the worst tragedies in sporting history. The plane he was to have been on, carrying the entire U.S. team, had crashed while landing at Brussels, leaving no survivors. Shocked by the tragic accident, the International Skating Union officials cancelled the 1961 World Championships.

The time spent in bed and the break from competition due to the cancellation of the World's gave Don the chance to review seriously his position in New York. Despite a satisfying Summer of skating Don began to feel the need for change. Pierre was one of the World's top coaches. He had given Don much to be thankful for. But in New York now there were no top competitive skaters he could train with. Carol Heiss, having won Olympic and World titles, had retired. Alain Giletti and Alain Calmat had returned to France. Don felt like a big fish in a small pond. Without the other stars to inspire him, he found himself going stale. Again, Don informed his parents that he wished to make a change. In Toronto there was a coach who had earned his respect. He would be closer to home. Finances would be easier. It all added up. He moved to Toronto to stay with his friends, the Beattys, and to join his new coach. . . .

5
Sheldon

The summer of 1961 brought with it a definite air of excitement. Don was in Oshawa preparing to leave for Schumacher, a small mining town in Northern Ontario. It would be his first season of skating under coach Sheldon Galbraith. Though the second time he'd made a major coaching change through his own wishes, Don felt no apprehension at the prospects for the future.

Schumacher, though only a small town in the middle of a busy mining district, had one of the biggest and most productive skating schools in Canada. When top coaches went there for the summer workouts, their top skaters followed, some being Sheldon's pupils: Senior Women's champion Wendy Griner, and pairs skaters Maurice Lafrance and Gertrude Desjardins. Don now would have again the kind of competition within the training environment that was missing from his spring training at New York.

With Don still in Oshawa, Sheldon sat staring at the ice surface of Schumacher's rink nearly 500 miles away and contemplated the imminent arrival of his new star pupil from Oshawa. He had first noticed Don's great talent six years earlier, in the Junior Men's championships of 1955. The young skater's brilliant, high-leaping double axels had particularly impressed him then. He had also seen room for improvement in Don's figures, even including the loop

Sheldon Galbraith

1962 Canadian Senior Champions—Virginia Thompson and William Mc-
Lachlan, Dance; Wendy Griner, Ladies; Donald Jackson, Men; Maria and
Otto Jelinek, Pairs

82

figure, which Don had actually won at that competition.

Now he would have a chance to play a part in what might be Don's final giant leap—the one to the top.

Sheldon was a perfectionist. He wanted all his pupils to have equal opportunity to improve. This he had already shown to Don the year before. Now as soon as Don and Wendy Griner arrived in Schumacher, he called them into his office.

He told the two young stars that a large part of the responsibility for having a good, productive school this summer lay on their shoulders. Younger skaters would watch how the "stars" practised. If Don and Wendy were to slacken off, the others would think that they too could achieve success in that manner. But if they went the other way, working their hardest, they would be invaluable assets. Both said they were ready to work.

In Don's case, the high star quality he had already displayed, along with his heavy artillery of jumps, now caused Sheldon to consider taking Don into new and unknown reaches of figure skating. He foresaw the development of an explosive and unpredictable routine that would keep judges and audiences alike on the edges of their seats.

As the first few days passed, Sheldon was impressed. Don showed dedication, and willingness to work. Sheldon thought maybe the little opening talk might have been unnecessary. However, he soon became troubled. Don showed a growing tendency to be his own boss. This might have been all right—except that the areas Don apparently felt needed work weren't the ones Sheldon saw.

For example, Sheldon felt that Don's skating technique sometimes caused him to have muscles fighting one another.

Balance needed to be achieved using the least line of resistance so that the balanced edge would put him into what Sheldon called a "spin centre". Rotation from a relaxed skating edge would leave various other muscles ready for action in a way that would generate a better lift into a jump. This in turn would help achieve a more controlled landing.

But Don was not working along these lines at all. Sheldon decided that the situation had to be dealt with immediately, without, if he could help it, endangering their rapport, or reducing Don's eagerness to get ahead—an invaluable aid to the learning process. So it was after much careful thought that he finally called Don in again.

This time Sheldon informed Don that there was one, and only one, kind of training situation that he was prepared to accept: one where the individual was developed by the trainer. At the same time, he did not want Don to be solely the development of his (Sheldon's) own conception. An individual might have his or her own ideas that might reach far beyond those of the coach. That "reaching beyond" was essential. So the coach's job was not to halt or stultify talent, but to get the most out of it by direction and development. With Don, whose long reach was known, all that had to be decided was who was doing the developing of that reach.

Sheldon was not through. He quickly followed his lecture on coaching philosophy by saying he realized how much Don had "knocked about" on his own, thereby perhaps establishing a greater self-understanding of his own skating. This undoubtedly meant that there was a great resource of thought to be tapped. Sheldon hoped that his pupil would continue to make himself heard—as long as it was within the kind of coach-student relationship that Sheldon had just laid out.

Don responded positively to the encounter. Coach and pupil then set to work discussing the various aspects of Don's skating that had to be improved if he were to become World Champion and fulfill his long dream. He had less than a year.

With the advanced level of skating involved, the work took on a much more technical nature. During the previous two years, Pierre had been concerned with developing Don's consistency in jumping. The focus had been on consistency in general. Now Sheldon wanted Don to move one particular jump up from its present seventy-five per cent consistency level to a ninety-five per cent level. The jump was the double axel. With their new understanding in mind, Sheldon left it up to Don to decide whether to be satisfied with things as they were or to change. Don took the challenge. That's when practices swung into high gear that summer in Schumacher.

After observing several of Don's double axels, Sheldon concluded that the problem lay not in the manipulation of the body during the jump or upon landing, but, rather, with the entrance to the jump. He set up a programme to correct that. He wanted Don to practise his preparation edge in such a way that he relaxed as he skated through the back edge, saving strength and power for the step onto the forward take-off edge and then the sudden lift off.

Wishing to restrict work to the entrance (and not having as convenient an excuse as Pierre), Sheldon simply forbade Don to do any double axels until his coach felt that it was time to do so. When Don said okay, he didn't know that he had six *weeks* of entrance work ahead before Sheldon would allow him to try another double axel.

But when the time did come, the coach's strategy paid dividends. Don found himself virtually assured of his double axel every time out. With this new found control, he decided to attempt his double axel in the way he had altered his single—keeping his arms in a crossed position. It meant doing two and a half revolutions in the air with the arms crossed. In that arm position, he was unable to provide any balancing effect from the preparation all the way through to the landing. To his delight, the new technique on the take-off edge increased the ease of rotation to such an extent that he landed the new jump on the very first try.

In spite of Don's high, leaping, and now, well-assured jumps, Sheldon was still not completely satisfied. He didn't like the way Don snapped his jumps around one after the other in lieu of having more spin rotation. A change there would be the final development in Don's jumping, from Ede's emphasis on body rhythm and reckless abandon, to Otto's desire for better posture and form, to Pierre's quest for not only more consistency but also a better understanding of the correlation between free skating and figures.

Sheldon knew that due to Don's tremendous body control and cat-like agility and reflexes, he could grab off landings where many others would have missed. And Don could still make such a salvaged jump look great. That was doing something well in spite of error. It was not what Sheldon wanted from his skater. In his view, a real world champion did something well because he had set up the situation himself with such skill that a poor outcome was impossible. To make that point with Don, Sheldon explained that he wanted Don to let his newly relaxed control and better balance work in tune with his natural rhythm and great reflexes, rather than using the latter elements as life-savers in times of stress. There would be greater control in the mid-air rotations and subsequent landings. As his coach spoke, Don nodded. A restaurant scene with a waiter drop-

ping plates off a tray passed fleetingly through his mind.

The work was hard. Don put in eight to nine hours of practice a day, five hours of figures and the rest in free skating. Twice a week he would do stroking work wearing the extra long blades of speed skates. Once in a while he had a dance session. With eating and sleeping, this turned into a twelve to thirteen hour day. It began at seven in the morning and left virtually no time for anything else. But then Schumacher was not exactly the hot bed of night life activity.

Summer is traditionally the time for a skater to work on new jumps, especially difficult ones. The thinking is that should an injury occur, a fracture or sprain, it would have time to heal before the winter's competitions. This prompted Sheldon to tell Don now that the time had come to begin perfecting what became the biggest bomb in the history of skating—the triple lutz jump.

Though deep down the coach felt that the triple lutz did not necessarily have to be a part of his pupil's programme in order for him to win the world championship, he knew it wouldn't hurt! Also he knew it was part of Don's reaching out, his total ambition. He wanted to become the first skater ever to have a triple lutz in his programme at an international competition. What coach in his right mind would try to stop him?

Don received the news enthusiastically. And it was probably his great enthusiasm that carried him through, because Sheldon had devised an unorthodox and quite painful prelude to his work on the big jump.

After watching his pupil try a few unsuccessful triple lutzes, Sheldon called him over and said, "Listen, Don. I want you to do your next attempt with your legs crossed like this." He indicated a body position about which Don was pretty doubtful. Eager as ever, Don skated out and tried it, finding his worst doubts confirmed as he crashed heavily to the ice—on his behind.

"Hmmmm—again," said Sheldon. Don, gingerly rubbing his sore spot, went back and tried again. Same result.

"Hummph," Sheldon grunted. He stared at the ice frowning. After a moment he murmured, "Again".

"*Again!?*"

"Again."

His pride now was hurting almost as much as his rear end, but Don once more leapt into the air in another attempt to do the jump correctly. The crash to the ice was even heavier than the previous two. And Don's pain level rose accordingly.

"*Great.*" was Sheldon's instantaneous exclamation. "I've just seen what I wanted to see. Now we can get to work on your triple lutz!"

As he lay there, Don didn't know whether to feel elated, furious or grateful for his coach's apparent revelation. However, he couldn't help smiling as he skated into position to start his next attempt. He never did find out just what it was that Sheldon had had to see at the expense of his own seating comfort over the next few days. At the end of the summer, Don landed his first clean triple lutz—three complete revolutions in the air followed by a one foot landing. He did it three more times before school finished.

Still, both Sheldon and Don remained cautious. It was well-founded. Don practised the triple lutz every day he could, all fall. That totalled over 500 trials. Yet, he did not land his fifth perfect triple lutz until Christmas. But he had been close many other times: three air revolutions with a two-footed landing; or two and three quarter revolutions in the air with the final quarter turn performed by the landing

foot on the ice surface. One promising note was the fact that he rarely fell attempting the jump.

The summer had gone well. Both student and coach were pleased about the progress in the free skating programme. This did not mean that the school figures had been disregarded or even put in a secondary light. On the contrary. Sheldon's general concern from the beginning had been the necessity of gaining the European acceptance for Don's skating. The judges there held the lion's share of the placing power. In Europe, school figures were No. 1 in importance. Sheldon knew that his pupil absolutely had to gain more respect for his school figures in relation to the people who were ahead of him in the world standings.

With summer school over in Schumacher, Don went to Lake Placid to skate in the Labour Day Carnival and also try his U.S. gold level dance test. This he did with U.S. Gold Dance competitor Dorothyann Nelson. After passing the test, he returned home for a brief visit and rest before his final season of skating in preparation for the 1962 World Championships.

In Toronto, Don found his coach ready to work on the entire five-minute free skating programme. This phase of the development would be geared to implanting more finesse into the in-between things (steps between stunts). Bombs alone, such as the triple lutz and delayed double salchow, would not be enough to carry a performance.

That made it time to work on Don's footwork. Sheldon smiled inwardly as he thought of the relatively easy task that lay before him. Don already had the fastest footwork of the day. However, all his movements were rotating ones. Sheldon hoped to complement them with a series of reciprocal movements. This would give his pupil's footwork two levels, one much quicker than the other. To Sheldon, the slow part of a programme was not a rest period for the skater. It had to be as strong as it could be.

With the initial work accomplished, Don was moving quickly and strongly on his feet in both directions while performing several intricate movements in a manner unequalled in the world. However, this was still not enough. Sheldon now wished to lengthen out some of Don's lines. He didn't want Don to sustain his movements over longer periods of time, but rather to extend his whole posture, compensating for his short limbs. These new extended lines of body position enabled Don to create the illusion of movement continuity while retaining the major asset of his footwork—his quickness.

With the basic programme parts now well developed, Sheldon turned his attention to the flow of the routine. The task of creating an innovative and technically superior free skating routine was made much easier by choosing what Sheldon considered to be excellent music. Don's 1958 programme music from the opera *Carmen* seemed even now to be almost exactly attuned to his artillery of movements on the ice, thanks to the painstaking care with which Pierre had put it together. Pierre was a perfectionist in music combinations and tape splicing, and had his own professional equipment for that purpose.

As far as Sheldon could determine, there were only a couple of sections where music bridges didn't allow the display of the variety of moves Don could offer. This was crucial. Sheldon knew that repetition, even at Don's high calibre, would not be conducive to winning scores at a competition where excitement was at its highest level. However, it appeared that only slight shadings of difference in skating to certain musical passages were needed to change the whole picture.

With no time left to start searching for better passages,

90

Sheldon and Don set about reworking the choreography leading into some sections that otherwise might appear to be repetitious.

One of the first things to be changed in the choreography was a pattern play in which Don always deked to his left before going to his right, while moving down the ice. The change involved setting up a series of new moves. These would appear to be leading into another pattern play, but due to Don's quickness and balance, instead would suddenly turn to a different direction with a slightly altered step. With this new flair in the routine, Don would be able to prevent judges from getting to know exactly what was coming, something they had been able to do before.

Other changes were made to freshen the programme. At one stop point in the 1957 programme, Don had used a lead-in step finished by a skid stop. Now, the step would be done with his hands on his hips, immediately followed by a double flip jump (with hands still on the hips), which then led to the skid stop.

There had also been at the end of the '57 programme a double lutz jump approached straight on. Sheldon helped Don formulate a unique entrance to the jump by having him skate with a straight edge, followed by a ninety degree turn which then introduced the jump.

All these things together seemed to give the programme its final necessary touches. At least it appeared that way to coach and student. Also, time had run out for preparation. Their first real test was upon them.

As the final week before the Canadian Senior Championships approached, Sheldon felt that Don was one of the most completely developed skaters going into the competition. With the admitted uncertainty of the triple lutz, he saw only the flying camel as a possible weakness in the programme. And even there, the only problem lay in the position of the spin. The jump, that was the most difficult part of the manoeuvre, was consistently good. However, everything did not go as easily as it might have.

With a flu virus running rampant throughout Europe, Don on his own had decided to take the necessary inoculation just before the Canadian Championships so he would be over its effects by the time he reached Europe for the World Championships—provided that he made the team. Although unwilling to admit anything of the sort to his coach, he felt sick for eight days before and during the Canadian competition. This was reflected in the way he skated.

Also, the day before the competition began, Sheldon and Don found that his music was being played at an incorrect tempo. As a result, one day they asked and received permission from the head referee to correct the situation.

Included in the permission the head referee had given them was a provision to go to the other competition rink and practice there because they had missed their own at Varsity Arena due to the music trouble. They took to the ice believing they had about twenty minutes. Such did not appear to be the case. An official ordered Don from the ice. He also backed Sheldon up against a wall complaining over what he believed was rudeness exhibited by coach and skater in attempting to stay on the ice.

Sheldon tried to quiet the official. He argued this was neither the time nor the place to have it out. However, Sheldon too became furious when told that he had no respect for the official's job. He had obligations to his skater, he said. The official also should show respect for the head referee's permission. After all, was the competition intended for the skaters, or not?

It all proved to be in vain. Don was forced to leave the ice.

The next day, Don skated in the competition and won—but it was not an easy win. He tried his triple lutz and his other triple jump, the triple salchow. In the first he didn't make the three revolutions, so he needed a two-footed landing. In the second he stumbled slightly over his toe pick on the landing.

Nevertheless, it was a win. That meant he would be able to go to Prague and take a shot at becoming what he had always hoped to be—World Champion.

But Sheldon was perplexed. Don had shown some of the flair that they had worked on, along with his usual strong performance. Sheldon felt that he should have been given at least a nodding approval for the skills he had presented. Such was not the case. In fact, one official from the Canadian Figure Skating Association remarked how he had heard how great the skaters were supposed to be, and asked why they hadn't been able to show it. Yet he had been one of the people responsible for the fouling up of Don's (and perhaps other) practice times.

With the Canadian championships behind him, Don was eager to get back to work right away on final preparation before the World's. Instead, Sheldon told him to take a couple of days off. This came as a total surprise to Don, but he accepted gratefully. It had been a long haul. The respite would help him shake the effects of the inoculation, as well.

Then it was time to leave for Prague. An infected toe had held up practice for a while but there had been nothing for him to do but perfect what was already there. The programme was complete. Now it was time to show it to the world.

Fans flock to the new Julius Fucik Stadium in Prague for the Championships

The draw for the skating order. Supervising the draw are Rudi Marx, Referee, and Alex Gordon, Assistant Referee

94

6

Prague

Pat sat down at the small table in the bedroom, opened a new notebook and began to write: "Sunday, March 4th— Left Toronto—George Gross at airport—took picture of Don getting on plane. Met . . .".

She paused and stared out the window at the twinkling skyline of New York City, thinking of the flight to New York; being met at the airport by Carol Heiss's father and his son, Bruce; dinner and the hospitality Mr. Heiss had shown in inviting her and Don to stay at his home.

The next day, Pat went with Don to visit his old friends at the Skating Club of New York. They all remarked that his jumps were higher than ever and his over-all skating much better than before.

Don stayed that night with the people who had taken him into their home before, the Coryns. There was much catching up to do. The hours before the focal point in a man's life sometime seem to drag. Next day, Tuesday, Don's departure was preceded by a going-away dinner. The festivities were extended unexpectedly when gale-force winds caused the flight to be delayed three hours.

The delay caused the Jacksons to miss their connection in Amsterdam. They spent the night there at the airline's expense; Wednesday they walked the canals, and had to spend another night in Amsterdam. Don was eager to be on his way. On Thursday, they flew to Zurich and then on to Prague. The biggest moment of Don's life was nearing.

Upon arrival, the Jacksons (along with another fine Canadian skater, Petra Burka, and her mother) were met by officials and driven directly to the International Hotel. It was modest-looking outside, which disguised the finely furnished rooms within. Most of the Canadian contingent was on the second floor. By five that day Don had settled into his room, unpacked his equipment and taken off for one of the practice rinks. It was having an open session of free skating of which Don wished to take advantage. He had missed a day's practice while in Amsterdam.

To his delight, Don found that the rink was virtually empty. Most other competitors had decided to arrive in Prague on Sunday, still three days away. When Don skated out, he was overwhelmed. Several thousand people had turned up solely to catch a glimpse of the great skaters going through their training sessions. With the effects of a long trip to overcome, Don concentrated on loosening up his muscles and getting the feel of the ice back into his feet and body.

The next day, Sheldon arrived along with Wendy Griner and her mother. He immediately put Don through a training session at the practice arena so rigorous that Don, very tired, turned down a chance to go and see the Czecho-slovakian Ice Revue that night in the new arena which was to be used for the world competition.

That day Don felt something wrong with one leg. In attempting his triple salchow, Don had felt some knee pain. The joint felt dry, as if parts were abrasively moving against each other. Don didn't tell Sheldon, but cut down to two or three triple salchows in each practice to rest the knee as much as possible. Fortunately the pain went away.

On Sunday, March 11th, Don took his first practice on

the ice of the new arena. He immediately glowed from ear to ear. His feeling for the texture of the ice was instantaneous. To him, it was almost ideal. Ten thousand people were in the rink for the free-skating workouts. Don responded by jumping as well as he had ever jumped before. Cameramen flocked around the skaters and sold the photos as postcards the next day. All of Don's, several thousand copies, had been all sold by the time Pat tried to buy one.

With all the skaters now in the city, both the practice rink and main rink were going full time with figures and free skating sessions. Sheldon was almost swamped with his schedule. There were times when Wendy and Don had practices at the same time, in different rinks. Sheldon then would handle only half of each pupil's workout. Between times, Sheldon sharpened his pupils' skates. At night he gave them powder massages as well. At first, Don had not taken to the massages. When he felt extra good in the next workout, however, he began to look forward to his rubdown after each skating session.

On Monday evening, March 12th, a reception was held at the town hall. The draw took place there for the men's figures starting positions. France's Alain Calmat was drawn third, Don fourth. Favourite Karol Divin of Czechoslovakia was to skate fifth. The competition was now only a day and a half away. The excitement was reflected in the crowds that swarmed to final practice sessions in both arenas.

Don's final workouts on Tuesday passed without incident. Sheldon, physically drained due to the rigorous schedule he had been keeping, kept a watchful eye not only on Don's skating but on his emotions. Both were fine. He realized that Don had been there before, knew exactly what was expected of him and, perhaps more importantly, knew what he was expecting of himself.

Don was expecting no less than his best. This was the culmination of all the years of hard work. As he lay in bed, he went over in his mind the four figures that he would have to do the next morning as part of the first day of competition. He could hardly wait to be out on the ice trying to match figures with his arch rivals Alain Calmat and Karol Divin.

Divin was going to be tough to beat. Not only was he the favourite, but he would be skating in front of a highly partisan home crowd. This crowd was sure to have at least a psychological influence on the judges. Still Don felt he must not think of beating anyone. The last time he had tried to beat someone it had cost him the world championship. He was here to do the best he was capable of doing. That just had to be good enough to win.

Wednesday morning, Don's first figure went well. He finished a close second to Divin. The same result occurred in the second figure. Things were looking good, so far, Sheldon thought. Don's free skating always could overcome any slight deficit in his figure scores. After the third figure, he was still very close to Divin in the point standings.

At that point, Sheldon, feeling contented with his pupil's efforts, wished him luck with the final figure. He had to leave and go to the practice rink. Wendy Griner was set to have her final workout before her competition began the next day. He felt no qualms about leaving Don. Maybe he couldn't have helped—but disaster was to strike on that last figure—a three-lobe that encompassed three circles with bracket turns in the ends.

In that fourth figure, Don was the last skater to use the patch before a shift would be made to clean ice. He had tried to use a clean piece of ice. The referees had told him

he had to stay on the ice the others had used. There was the added complication that the dirty ice was on an end patch. Due to this, previous skaters had stayed within a limited part of the patch as far as possible away from the end boards. The dilemma facing Don now was whether to skate on the very dirty part of the patch away from the boards or go with the cleaner ice closer to them. He decided on the latter.

Slightly flustered, Don began to lay out his figure. Subconsciously he must have followed the curvature of the boards. When he went to trace his figure, he realized that one of his circles had been laid a foot and a half off the centre line of the other two. His first impulse—to try to correct his mistake—proved to be a double error. The judges might not give him credit for his tracing, but he was now emphasizing by his attempted correction the glaring error he had made originally. This tactical error set him back a whopping thirty-five points behind Divin. It also nearly caused Sheldon to have a heart attack when he heard the news.

As Don skated from the ice, he knew the trouble, even wreckage, he had wrought to himself. The only judge he saw as he left was Britain's Pam Davis. She looked disappointed and disgusted. Pierre's words from long ago suddenly floated through his mind: "If you go by the mark you get from Davis, you'll have a pretty good idea of what you've done on the ice." She had put him well down on that figure. There had been simply no way for her to hold him up.

Though disappointment clearly showed in his face, inwardly Don was telling himself, "Today is over, it's time to concentrate on tomorrow". However, it didn't work. He was beside himself with frustration. Others could see it. His former teammate from New York, Alain Calmat of France, skated over. Tapping Don gently on the shoulder, he said, "You know, Don, you've got another day. You can do it. You've got two more figures. You've got your free skating. Don't worry."

Don felt a sudden surge of warmth and respect towards his French friend. This was what sport was all about. Here was a fellow competitor consoling him when that competitor was right behind him in the standings—just because they were friends. And though Don felt he would have done the same for this or another friend, Don never forgot Calmat's gesture. But he still wished he hadn't been so obvious in letting his emotions run away.

Don dressed quickly. He wanted to eat and get to bed early in preparation for the next day's competition. He was so depressed and tired that he decided to miss the night session at the rink, featuring finals of the pairs competition, even though Canada had a good shot at a medal. Maria and Otto Jelinek were rated with the best in the world.

Although Maria fell during the performance, she and Otto skated well enough to win. Canadians in attendance went wild with jubilation. Talk at the reception that night revolved around the gold medal already secured—and the one that was about to be, the next day, by Don Jackson. His poor showing in the first four figures had not curbed the confidence everyone had in his abilities as a champion skater.

At 5:45 a.m. Don awoke. He looked across the room at the sleeping form of Otto Jelinek. How had he and Maria done? Don wanted to wake Otto and ask, but didn't. Then, dressing, he happened to glance over to Otto's dressing chair. His heart leapt to his throat. There at the end of a long green ribbon, hung a shiny *gold* medal! He rushed

across the room and read the inscription on the ribbon: "First Place—World Championships".

An intensity of feeling such as Don had never before experienced swept through his body. He charged over and shook Otto.

"Otto! Otto! congratulations, you won!" were the first words. Then came a barrage of questions and comments. Otto barely stirred. Finally he opened his eyes to see Don's sparkling eyes and ear-to-ear grin. "Oh yeah, thanks a lot," he mumbled. "Now let me sleep." Then, as Don quietly began to leave, Otto opened his eyes again. "Oh, by the way, Don, good luck today," he called. The small retreating figure turned, smiled and murmured thanks, then slipped out.

Though the victory reception for Otto and Maria had lasted until three in the morning, Pat was up and waiting to see her son when he came down to breakfast. She was overjoyed to find him in good spirits and full of determination to do his best in the figures still remaining so that he might still have a chance to pull out the victory in the free skating part of the competition.

The fifth figure to be skated was the loop. Don took to the ice full of confidence. Sheldon looked on from the stands in mild disbelief at this apparent show of confidence and then practically jumped out of his seat in a rage when he observed his star pupil pull out some analysis sheets right on the ice and begin to study them. Though Don's back was turned to the judges, it was clear for everyone to see that he was looking at some sort of note paper which he then stuffed into his pockets just before performing the figure.

The notes were little analysis sheets that Sheldon had made up for his pupil showing his normal pattern of errors. Don had reasoned that by looking at them just before he skated, he would be less likely to make one of his "usual" errors. Sheldon wanted to throw a rock at him. His anger was soon appeased. Don skated an excellent figure. However, the judges still gave a slight advantage to Karol Divin. The sixth and final figure was also well done. Don had given up only ten points to Divin over the course of the last two figures. This in itself was a great achievement. However, coupled to the previous day's scores, Don was 45 points behind Divin going into the free skating portion. Too many points. Almost impossible to surmount. But they'd soon find out.

At the completion of the compulsory figures, the draw to determine the skating order for that night's final was made. Sheldon and Don were both very pleased with the result. Divin was to skate 12th, Don 16th, Calmat 18th. This meant that Don would know exactly what he needed to do to overcome Divin's lead, if that could be done without a miracle.

With the draw completed and a delay before the dance competition, the skaters were given twenty minutes of ice time to practise their routines. Don quickly took advantage. It meant he would not have to travel all the way to the other rink to practise later that afternoon. Instead, he'd rest and eat at a leisurely pace before the final.

As he had done so many times in the past, Don leapt to the ice to free skate and forget all the pressures that had built up around him. Without really concentrating on anything at the outset, he sped about the ice and relieved the pressure and tenseness that had been with him during the figures. There was no need to skate hard. He would do that later on. But after several minutes, he tried a few of his jumps and other manoeuvers. Everything flowed smoothly.

He left the ice eager to meet the challenge facing him that night.

One of the last things he had attempted—and missed—was the triple lutz. Doing the jump just for feel, he had not worried over the miss. It was to be part of his programme, period. He had told everyone that there would be a triple lutz in his routine. The judges would be looking for and expecting it; the first skater in history to include that jump in an international competition.

At the hotel, Sheldon called Don to his room. He realized that Don was going to be nervous. He didn't want Don to be alone or even alone with his coach. So Maurice Lafrance was also there. Sheldon knew Lafrance's good disposition, his ability to say the right things, keep it light, keep Don's concentration away from the competition for as long as possible. Along with that, Sheldon also administered a light massage to Don's body to help tone his muscles.

When Sheldon decided to have a meal brought up to the room, Don made no special request. The three gathered around the table. Discussion finally turned to the final. Sheldon felt that the time was now right to discuss strategy.

From sources close to the judges, Sheldon had heard that Don was being viewed in a favourable light after his resurgence in the second set of compulsory figures. The question which had to be settled now, Sheldon thought, was the triple lutz. Sheldon felt that the jump was now no longer absolutely necessary. Don could win without it. The risk of injury if the jump were missed was great. What if that affected the rest of what could be a flawless programme?

Even as he spoke Sheldon sensed his pupil's reaction. His

feelings were confirmed. Don said, "I'm going to do the jump." However, after more conversation, he relented—a little. He promised to leave the jump out if he felt really bad in his warm-up or in the approach to the jump once the programme was underway. Sheldon was a little more relaxed. He was willing to take personal responsibility for omitting the triple lutz. To him, trying the jump would be throwing caution to the wind, with really no need to do so.

They talked some more. The competition battleground as Sheldon saw it had switched from the ice into the air—a place where Don was much more at home than Divin. That should give Don confidence with or without the triple lutz.

Don responded well. Maurice kept things easy. Don decided to go to his room to rest. Sleep was an impossibility. Time seemed to stand still. He thought over his performance again and again. Then he was on the bus, headed for the rink, Sheldon beside him. Sheldon now wanted to take Don's mind off his actual performance and yet keep it on skating. He discussed with Don the results given by individual judges during the compulsory figures. They analysed the cases in which it would be mathematically possible for Don to pull up, and those cases in which it would be very difficult or impossible. This helped pass the time on the bus. Don walked into the arena not having had time to think or get nervous about the triple lutz or anything else.

In the dressing room, Don laced his skates with care. His thoughts wandered out to the ice surface. Divin was in the midst of his free skating performance. However, Don had no desire to go out and observe the judges' marks for Divin's routine. He did not want anything to interfere with his own preparation. If he'd gone out and had seen Divin get a set of 5.9's, realizing that those marks spelled the end of his chances to win, it might have dampened his spirits, reduced his effectiveness on the ice. When he took to the ice for his warm-up, he was completely in the dark as to how Divin had done, and did not ask.

This warm-up was to be no different than any other he had done before. Much loosening up had already been done in the dressing room. All that was left to do was get the feel of the ice. Don liked to start out by skating leisurely around the ice looking for the high and low spots and the general condition of the surface. Once this was done, he went into his first movement which he had learned from Gus Lussi— a sit spin to help the blood circulate and begin to stretch his muscles. After further stretching movements in a stationary position, he skated around slowly, throwing in several of his easy jumps to get the feel of the take-offs and landings. His smile was growing more radiant by the minute. Ice conditions were near ideal. He then began to go through all the jumps that he would be using in the routine. The practice jumps were done in the general area they would be done in the actual performance but not in the exact spot; Don did not want to do actual take-offs on top of the practice ones. All the jumps were feeling good to him. He decided to attempt his triple lutz, but without putting everything he had into it. He was still just looking for the feel of everything. He approached the jump and leapt up and around for two and three-quarter revolutions, landing with a quarter-turn cheat and touching his free foot down to maintain his balance. It had felt so smooth that his grin went from ear to ear. He looked up into the crowded stands at Sheldon and flashed an "OK" sign with his hand as he prepared to leave the ice. Sheldon quickly responded with his thumb in the air and Don knew that he had received the consent of his coach to go ahead and try the triple lutz in the competition.

Sheldon, meanwhile, was pleased that Don had been calm enough to remember to indicate how well he felt after the warm-up. As he was getting ready to go down and join Don, he was greeted by Melville Rogers, a Canadian judge who was not involved in the judging of the competition. Sitting nearby, he had noticed the exchange of signals between Sheldon and Don.

Rogers asked increduously, "You're not *really* going to let that young man do the triple lutz in his performance, are you? You'd be crazy if you did! It's just not worth taking the chance. You know it."

With a slight smile, Sheldon answered mildly, "If Don wants to do it, it's his programme—therefore he can do it." Then he hurried towards the dressing room.

When he arrived in the locker area, Sheldon was taken slightly aback. Don was gazing intently at one of the washroom walls. Then Sheldon saw what had Don's attention riveted to the wall. He'd taken out a pocket-sized eight-millimetre projector and was showing himself films of his past performances in the routine he'd be doing again in a few minutes. It was his last chance to cue his mind to the various positions, timing aspects and approaches involved. Most importantly, it gave him a final mental review of the body movements in sequence to the music he would follow. He wanted to ensure that there would be no repetition of what happened long ago at West Point when his mind had gone blank on his music and he'd adlibbed his routine.

After a few moments of discussion, Sheldon once more offered Don an out on the triple lutz. "You don't have to do it if you don't feel absolutely right about doing it tonight."

Don looked up from the bench. He was re-lacing his skates. "I am going to do it," he said!

When it was time to go out. Don drew a deep breath and let it out slowly. He rose and firmly strode to the door of the dressing room. Sheldon followed close behind. The twosome began its short trek down the corridor to rinkside. Swarms of photographers swooped in with flashbulbs going off like machine gun fire. Sheldon whipped in front of Don, imploring that no more pictures be taken. He told Don to shield his eyes. "Don't let a flash catch you. It'll take several minutes for your eyes to readjust to the regular lighting . . ." Minutes. Don knew he would be finished with his programme in minutes.

Whether this whole byplay was a psychological ploy by Sheldon to get his skater's mind off the imminent start of his performance Don did not know. It did keep his mind off the competition during those last few seconds of waiting while the skater just in front of him received his marks.

Then came the signal for Don to head out onto the ice. Don turned quickly toward his coach. He never used Sheldon's first name. In a quiet voice, he asked, "Mr. Galbraith, *is* there a chance that I could pull up?"

Sheldon knew Karol Divin's scores. He had received high 5.7's for his programme. That meant Don would need virtually all perfect marks, sixes, to overcome the 45-point deficit. Sheldon looked his pupil square in the eye and quietly replied, "Don, there's room at the top".

"Thank you, Mr. Galbraith, that's all I wanted to know." Don turned and stepped onto the ice.

During the competition—the greatest free skating performance of all time

Another part of Don's free skating program—9 judges and 18,000 people watching in the Stadium, and an estimated 250,000,000 watching it live on Eurovision

7

King

"This is Donald Jackson of Canada. He is 21 years old. If he is going to win the World Championship tonight, and many people have expected him to do it, he must give the greatest performance of his life." The words were those of ABC-TV sportscaster Jim MacKay. They were being broadcast to millions. Viewers in Canada and the United States watched the trim figure of Don as he stood at centre ice waiting for his music to begin. In the Fucik Sports Hall 18,000 pairs of expectant eyes were trained on him. Only he had any chance to beat Karol Divin, their local hero. The World Championship was about to be won—or lost.

Don took a couple of long, deep breaths to clear his lungs. He looked up for a brief moment. Pat, hands clenched, knew he was about to say a silent prayer. As he looked back down, a smile began to spread across his face. The introductory part of his programme music began to play from the loudspeakers. There was total silence in the arena except for the music. Don spread his arms and took his first step.

That first step let the judges and everyone else know that Don was indeed going to take the battle into the air. He lifted off from that first step into a forward one-turn jump and then did a bunny hop to start himself on his way. He built up speed as he angled across the width of the ice and then cut left gaining more speed as he rounded the first corner.

The crowd was expectant. The millions of TV viewers knew from the commentary of former world champion Dick Button of the U.S., working with ABC, that Don was going to open his programme with the three revolutions from a lutz position. It would be the first ever in world competition if he succeeded.

Don's mind was not concerned with the success of the jump itself, but, rather, with the mechanics of it. Half-way along the end boards he pivoted into a backward position, which he held as he headed back up the ice along the boards. His mind began to race. The biggest moment of his life was just seconds away.

Rhythm, which had always been the key in Ede's coaching, was Don's main concern as his smooth crosscuts gave him increasing momentum. His rhythm was building—building on the natural lilt he felt developing from the sheer excitement of the way he was skating, and from his music.

He reached the imaginary centre line of the rink and began to angle away from the boards towards his original starting point, gliding backward on his right skate. His body position was nearly upright. His thoughts went to the deep knee bend he'd need to get the next important prerequisite for the take-off—balance. His ankles must be solid. Even a slight give or twist could cause an injury. That had happened twice before—once while practising the triple lutz with Pierre, and once later with Sheldon. Don had to make sure that the ice wasn't going to chip away from his toeing foot, which he would be implanting into the ice at the end of his glide. If at that final instant the toe hold wasn't perfect, he would have to back away from the triple lutz and do a mere double instead—something he did not wish to do. To maintain perfect balance, he would have to make

110

sure that he didn't push off too hard either with his toeing foot or his skating one. Due to the severe counter-rotation of the upper body he would have to attain to complete three revolutions in the air, it was necessary to hold his balance on the ice just a shade longer than if he were only doing the double.

His final concern was separation of the legs on take-off and in the air. Don performed his jump with his legs together. This meant he had to separate his legs on take-off by as much as 18 inches. The spin pull would then be brought about by forcing his legs together in the air. This required phenomenal strength and agility.

All these thoughts came and went within the brief time it took Don to glide in from the boards to centre ice. Now his mind cleared to deal with the physical situation at hand. He bent his right knee so that his body and extended left leg were almost parallel to the ice surface. Then he straightened his body as his left leg swung down and prepared to touch the ice for the take-off.

For everyone in the arena the world stopped turning. Pat closed her eyes and said a silent prayer. Millions of television viewers heard nothing but the background music from *Carmen* as Jim MacKay and Dick Button watched in silence.

Don's left toe touched the ice. He balanced for a split second. This was the moment everyone was waiting for. The media had made it known that Don would attempt the elusive and enormously difficult triple lutz. Don couldn't back away now. Neither did he want to. He sprang into the air with his feet apart, arms perpendicular to his body.

Spinning almost faster than the eye could follow, he brought his feet together and his arms into his chest as his body continued to rise.

A roar that would have made the walls of Jericho tumble echoed through the arena. Tears welled in Pat's eyes. Canadians in the stands hugged one another. Millions more back home heard Dick Button's confirmation of the historic feat: *"A beautiful triple lutz! It's fantastic!"*

Don had landed cleanly on his left foot with his arms again extended perpendicular to his body. His free right leg had swung around his body into the landing position. With the tension of the Triple Lutz cleared away, Don told himself it was time to enjoy skating the routine.

It was a good thing he adopted this relaxed psychological attitude. The deafening roar of the crowd showing appreciation of the Triple Lutz was drowning out his music. By the time Don could hear it again from the loudspeakers, he had skated around the end of the rink doing two complete turns and then stepping to his back edge before heading down the length of the ice doing reverse half and full turns.

In the stands Sheldon's face was a picture of relief. He nudged Melville Rogers, a Canadian figure skating judge, and said: "I told you he could do it, didn't I?" In his excitement Sheldon's camera moved and instead of shots of Don, he was shooting the ceiling. Sheldon was elated that Don managed to land his sixth ever triple lutz when it really counted. But elation soon gave way to concern that his pupil would draw a blank after achieving the historic milestone. Don's having to skate to music from memory for a few seconds had been the big test as far as Sheldon was concerned. Then the music could be heard again. Don had come through. But still more than 80 per cent of his routine was to come.

Don was satisfied. "Boy, I landed it perfectly," he said to himself. "And the audience loved it. Everything seems to

be going well. The ice conditions are good, my metabolism is just right and I feel great. I can't let up, though. I still have one big jump left—the triple salchow. I have to land that one perfectly, too."

As he neared the opposite end, Don moved back to a forward position to accelerate on the corners, then angled out of the second corner towards centre ice. Again gliding briefly, this time on his right leg, he bent his knee, leaving his left leg extended. From there he did a three turn on his skating foot. The left leg swung through to stay behind. Smoothly, his left toe came down and propelled him in the air for two revolutions of the double flip jump. Another clean landing on his left foot was greeted with more applause. Such a tremendous beginning brought unbounded elation to the hearts of millions of Canadians, who may have thought the impossible had already been accomplished. Such, however, was not the case. The words of Jim MacKay brought viewers back to the harsh reality Don was facing.

"Karol Divin is leading," emphasized MacKay. "If Jackson can give one of the great performances, well, I should say of all time, he can win—otherwise he cannot. As a matter of fact, looking at our unofficial figures here, it looks as if Jackson would have to have marks of either 5.9 or 6.0, which is perfection, from almost every judge in order to have even a chance of catching Divin. It's almost impossible."

However, "impossible" was not a word in Don's vocabulary. He was simply skating his heart out. From the landing of the double flip jump, he showed a hint of his flashy footwork as he skated back to centre ice, turned around to his left back edge and took off, making a full revolution before landing on his left foot. Gliding on his landing leg, he introduced the right rhythm into his body by taking a two-count knee bend and followed his first walley jump with yet another, this time landing on the other foot to use the move in preparation for the double salchow. He landed it splendidly and the crowd gave him a thunderous ovation.

He smiled, and skated the length of the rink, then cut to his right to make the turn at the corner. He followed the boards to mid-ice, turned on his back edge and began to cross-cut to the other side. Gliding backward on his left blade as he turned up the ice, he turned forward again, stepped onto his right forward edge for the take-off into the two and a half revolutions of the double axel jump before landing on his left foot. The crowd again roared its approval.

Not giving the fans a chance to stop cheering, Don stepped forward and did a three-turn en route to another clean double axel, landing on his left foot. The crowd gasped, then exploded with a spontaneous ovation in appreciation of the back-to-back double axels.

The landing of the double axels added to Don's confidence, but he knew he couldn't let up. He remembered that in going through the programme with Sheldon it wasn't only being able to skate the program, but also knowing how and where to pace himself that was essential.

Don paused to show the change in the tempo of his music and then, with a big smile, pushed off smoothly on his right leg. He picked up speed, heading towards the end of the rink. Near the corner he turned backwards, sped around the end boards, then angled out towards centre ice to get a forward position, in a manner that became known as the Jackson step. And again the crowd applauded, this time for his intricate technique.

And Don gave them more. Midway along the boards he cut to his right to head up the ice doing a half turn on his

left foot to skate backward. This was followed by successive half turns to a forward right and then back to a backward left skating position. At that point he placed his hands on his hips while gliding.

With hands still on his hips, Don stepped forward to his right foot, used it as a pivot, turned around to his back edge and took off into his second double flip. It was a variation of the jump, a variation never before seen in world skating competition. He landed cleanly on his left foot, hands still on hips. Scarcely touching the ice, travelling backwards, he hopped back in the air and turned his right skate sideways upon landing to effect a skidding stop to match his music as it also slid into a break point.

Don was by then half way through the programme. The crowd, the judges and his rivals felt they were witnessing figure skating's all-time great free skating performance. And there were still two and a half minutes of it left.

The two single axels that followed whetted everybody's appetite. He landed one in opposite direction from the other, and the crowd cheered again. After landing the second axel he made a semi-circle glide before he turned forward onto his left leg, hopped up with both feet in the air and made a dead-stop, two-point landing as the music once more paused for an instant.

Don heard the applause, but did not acknowledge it. He was concentrating on the next sequence, which was very important because of its interpretive character. "Concentrate hard, Don," he said to himself.

He did a loop on the spot before turning slightly and pushing off as the introduction to the *Habanera* passage from *Carmen* started up. He had to hit it right because in the ensuing seconds his steps had to correspond with the beat of the music. Interpretation of the music is one aspect of a skater's performance to which judges pay close attention. Three small jumps were part of this segment.

With long strides Don wound his way down the length of the ice before repeating the glide with his inside leg swung to the outside of the skating foot. However, instead of shifting to a back position as before, he leaped a complete revolution, landing on his left forward edge and heading across the width of the ice. That was another Jackson innovation. Again the crowd cheered wildly.

Reaching the corner, he turned to his back edge, picking up speed as he rounded the end boards and angled towards centre ice. Gliding forward on his right blade, he turned backward and then extended his free left leg to its fullest behind his body. He was preparing to execute a delayed double salchow, a jump he introduced in the 1958 World Championships at Paris.

From this position he vaulted again, this time appearing to hang in mid-air. With apparent ease, Don nimbly spun not once but twice to complete a delayed double salchow jump before landing on his left skate. The crowd ooh'd and ah'd, clapping all the time.

Gliding backward after the jump, Don folded his arms at shoulder level and skated a semi-circle which took him from the boards at centre to the middle. He moved back into the corner, and with his arms still folded took off to do two and a half revolutions in completing yet another double axel, one that showed balance and control and made more difficult by his folded arms. The crowd thrilled to yet another exclusive Jackson jump.

And still there was more. Taking long glides, Don used half turns in semi-circles to progress the length of the ice, still interpreting the *Habanera* with a one-foot axel which led into a flying camel and spin.

Don spun faster as he pulled himself into a tight upright position, then amazed everyone by seemingly spinning right off the ice and back down again. Once again the crowd roared its appreciation and clapped thunderously as Don used the momentum on his spinning landing to do a half circle before coming around and heading down the ice.

At centre he stopped, took a stride back up the ice, cut to his left to the side boards, and cut once again to his left to head down ice. The music began to pick up speed. So did Don. He stepped forward, leaped, and quickly tucked one and a half revolutions away to complete the delayed axel. There were 90 seconds remaining on his five-minute programme. To that point it had been flawless.

That's when the triple salchow flashed into his mind. "I know I can do it," he said to himself. "But I mustn't be overconfident. Everything has been going so well, let's keep plugging away. It can't be long now. Concentrate, Don, concentrate."

He headed across the ice and cut left, then backwards around the corner, around the end boards before heading up ice along the side. Nearing centre ice he angled towards the point of his Triple Lutz, gliding on his left leg. He turned and stepped onto his right leg, did a right forward three-turn and soared high for his second triple jump. A clean landing on his left foot signalled the spectacular completion of the triple salchow.

However, before Dick Button had finished exclaiming, "Beautifully done!" and before the spectators had time to applaud, Don stepped back off his glide. He flew into the air in a tucked position to do a flying sit spin, landed cleanly, still spinning. He straightened from his sit spin into

Still in good shape right after his history-making performance. The interview with Dick Button and the announcement of the marks are yet to come

an upright spin while the crowd continued to applaud almost in disbelief.

Now he stopped. There was just under a minute remaining. He knew he must increase his concentration. It had been a great performance but his air battle was not over. With each jump providing the possibility of a fall, he could not afford to let down even for a split second.

The double loop was next and Don executed it flawlessly. He had never fallen in a world championship and he was now confident he wouldn't ruin his perfect record.

He began skating with typical Jackson steps, the very steps some people had laughed about when Don had introduced them. He took off on a double toe loop, and landed it cleanly at the middle of the end boards to another thunderous ovation from the fans. The excitement in the stands grew as he headed into his last 30 seconds and a final double lutz. Relaxed, beaming, and showing no signs of fatigue, Don started to build momentum.

Reaching centre, he glided backward on his right foot. With a bend at the waist and a slight turn of his skate, he curved his glide on a 90-degree angle to the middle of the ice past the judges.

He then bent deeply at the knee, bringing his head close to his skating foot before taking off with his arms folded on his chest. They were still crossed after the two revolutions of the double lutz. The ovation had barely begun again when he stepped forward onto his right leg and, with arms still crossed, took off for one and a half more revolutions of an axel which brought him down cleanly going backwards on his left skate.

The crowd continued to clap and shout as Don stepped

The winners of the 1962 World's: 1st—Donald Jackson, 2nd—Karol Divin, 3rd—Alain Calmat

The Victory Parade

around to his forward edge. He rounded the end boards and turned to his left in the corner. Once more he stepped forward on his right leg and jumped high, legs neatly crossed over during the axel, and he landed cleanly.

The adrenalin was flowing as Don cut to the middle for his closing move. *"Look at the smile on his face as he goes into his final spin!"* exclaimed Dick Button. As Don came up from his sit spin into a swift upright spin, the music stopped. So did Don, and a roar went up in the Fucik Sports Hall that drowned all inner thoughts.

Pat's eyes welled and her heart pounded thunderously. Looking about, she was surprised to see tears flowing from the eyes of hundreds of Czechoslovakian spectators. They gave the young skater from Canada a standing ovation. It lasted fifteen minutes. They sensed that what they had seen had been the greatest performance in skating history.

What a programme it had been! Besides Don's intricate footwork along with his spins, there had been a remarkable total of 22 jumps: two triples (including the first-ever Triple Lutz), ten doubles (one of which was delayed) and ten singles (all of which had slight variations, including one delayed). On the average, Don had performed a jump every 13 seconds for five minutes. It was all accomplished effortlessly; many of the jumps just seemed to happen, with no noticeable preparation.

The question remaining was whether the judges had seen the performance in the same spectacular light. Don needed very high marks to overcome his point deficit. That fact was in everyone's mind, except Don Jackson's. As he bowed to the roaring audience, he felt totally pleased with himself. He had accomplished the Triple Lutz. He had skated to the

Don in post-championship exhibition for the press

The Champion takes off . . .   . . . and lands!

(Pictures taken for the press after the championships)

very best of his ability. Somehow it no longer mattered how the judges saw it. He had achieved what he had desired of himself. This attitude manifested itself when he was cornered by Dick Button for an interview.

"We have Don Jackson here at the rinkside while we are waiting for his marks," Button said. "The audience is roaring its approval. Congratulations, Don, on the greatest performance of your career!" It was impossible for Button to contain his enthusiasm.

"Thank you very much," replied Don. "I was really pleased."

Button said, "You had a smile on your face from ear-to-ear."

"After that Triple Lutz," Don said, "I think I'd have it anytime."

"I think that was the greatest jump I have ever seen," Button said.

Suddenly, there were the marks: "5.9; 5.8; 5.9; 5.9; 5.9; *there's a six!*" cried Jim MacKay, "5.9; 5.9; and 5.9! One 5.8, everything else 5.9 or 6!"

Pat gasped and, after seeing the third judge's marks, gave up trying to figure out where Don stood. Sheldon just sat and stared.

Once more the voice of Jim MacKay alerted the viewers: "Here comes the second set. *A six!* a 5.8! *another six! another six!* 5.9; *another six!* 5.9; *a six! and another six!!*"

It was incredible. Pat felt she must be dreaming. Sheldon was delighted, and then he was congratulated by friends sitting nearby. All were dumbfounded. Don had received seven 6's!

1.

2.

3.

1. Ljudmila Belousova and Oleg Protopopov of the USSR—silver medalists in the 1962 World's. They went on to win 4 World and 2 Olympic championships

2. Virginia Thompson and William McLachlan of Canada—bronze medallists in the 1962 World's

3. Dorothyann Nelson and Pieter Kollen of the USA—United States Senior Pair Champions and runners-up in the US Dance Championship; 8th in World Pairs and 7th in World Dance in 1962. Two of the very few skaters who have ever qualified to skate in more than one event at a World Championship

"I think without a doubt it's the greatest number of 6's ever given", commented Button, gazing at the judges' cards.

"Thank you very much, Dick," answered Don. "I'm very glad I could do it for Canada."

Then Button motioned to Don to take a bow at centre ice. Don declined. He felt such a gesture would upstage other competitors who hadn't yet skated. He quickly turned towards the dressing room.

Jim MacKay summed up the situation: "The result is still in doubt—remember that—he needed to get these great marks to have a chance of catching Karol Divin. When the results are announced we are going to see a tremendous moment here at this stadium."

However, it was under the stands, unseen by anyone, that perhaps the great moment of the championships took place. After Don had waved to him while being interviewed, Sheldon had been so overcome with emotion, he'd stayed away for awhile to leave Don alone in the dressing room. As Don relaxed, the door opened and Karol Divin entered. "Don, I know that the competition is very close," he said. "I would like to tell you that if I win I wish to give my gold medal to you. You were the greatest one in this competition."

Don was deeply moved. He murmured a choked-up thanks and shook his rival's hand warmly. By the time Don had collected himself and returned to the rink, the competition had ended.

The announcement would be in the native language only. Pat sat restlessly waiting for it. And then it came, and her Don was the Champion of the World. She closed her eyes

Exhibitions the day after the championships at Prague. 250,000 people were turned away from this sell-out performance. L to R: Maria and Otto Jelinek, Eva and Pavel Roman, Sjoukje Dijkstra, Donald Jackson

The two Dons—successive World Champions for Canada—Don Jackson 1962, Don McPherson 1963

in thanks as she heard the name of her son, accompanied by a thunderous roar of approval.

Don had done it! With his marvellous performance, he had come from behind to edge Karol Divin. His grin flashed as he mounted the podium to receive his medal. Ardent applause came from the man waiting next in line, Karol Divin. Don's old team mate, Alain Calmat, was third. Afterwards, the three skaters circled the rink wearing their medals and carrying flowers. Don, unable to see his mother and thinking the other two would give away their flowers, handed his flowers to Dorothyann Nelson, a U.S. skater he had dated. Then to his chagrin, he saw the other two give their flowers to their mothers. But as it was the only mistake he'd made all night, Pat forgave him.

When the three completed their victory skate, photographers asked for action shots. Don did some flying sit-spins and on the third one concentrated on the pose for the photographers. It was great. However, with his concentration diverted from the total mechanics of the jump, Don landed on his behind on the ice. The audience roared with laughter, then applauded when Don shrugged to indicate even he can't win 'em all.

Don finally got to the hotel for the Canadian celebration party. During it the phone rang. Long distance from Oshawa. It was radio station CKLB. Don and Pat talked. Pat wistfully mentioned how nice it would be to talk to George and Bill. Soon CKLB called back. George and Bill were in the studio. George had heard the news driving home. At home he found Bill in a frenzy. His son was sick with excitement and George was too. The call was the best

Toronto Telegram

The Homecoming—Oshawa, April 1962

The car presented to Don by the City of
Oshawa and some of their sports-minded
businessmen—can he keep it? (Nigel Stephens,
CFSA President, in the background)

medicine for both. As Don talked, Karol Divin, standing nearby, grabbed the phone and yelled across the Atlantic: "He was fantastic."

With a little champagne and the release of the day-long tension, Don slipped upstairs to his room and went to sleep. Before falling asleep, he looked up and saw the long green ribbon with a gold medal over his chair. . . .

After the competition Don learned the holiday would be brief. Skaters had been assembled to tour Europe, beginning with Prague itself.

The tour took them to Davos, Cologne, Copenhagen, Amsterdam, Dusseldorf and neighbouring towns. Don found himself doing three and four encores. He cut his routine to four minutes so he could devote the fifth minute to encores. Then he'd be coaxed to do consecutive jumps while the audiences counted. Sometimes he'd do 25 axels, or six double axels with three turns between, and still the audience didn't want to let him go. To top that, he attempted his Triple Lutz at every performance. It had been part of his winning routine. He didn't want to disappoint audiences.

Finally, Don was ready for home. He flew to Boston to fulfill a commitment to the skating-show people who had paid his way to and from the World Championships. Then it was back home to Oshawa.

Upon his arrival Don was put into a new convertible, inching its way to city hall while 15,000 Oshawans shouted appreciation. The mayor informed Don the car was his. Being an amateur, Don could accept gifts only if the retail value was under $50.

Next Don faced the dilemma of whether to turn professional. Should he begin repaying his parents for their financial sacrifices? Or should he remain amateur for two more years and try to win an Olympic gold?

The big ice shows approached Don and his parents. It was a difficult decision. Then Otto and Maria Jelinek invited Don to accompany them to Portugal for a holiday after an exhibition in Berlin. Don needed the holiday and time to relax and think about his future. He accepted.

But, for the moment, even that was unimportant.

Now, he would gaze upon the long green ribbon with the gold medal hanging in his bedroom in Oshawa. His face would break into that characteristic ear-to-ear grin. And he'd say to himself: "The first ever Triple Lutz in world competition; World Champion—my dream a reality."

"Me First" had done it. . . .

Epilogue

I

The exhibition in West Berlin was over. Don journeyed to Portugal with the Jelineks for a much-needed vacation. However, many people—representatives of the various ice shows—wanted him to keep his mind on skating even during his holiday. They knew Don would be a big draw, and they were making competitive offers for his services.

The first decision for Don, was not which show to choose, but, rather, whether to choose a show at all. After serious deliberation with friends, officials, and coaches, he decided to turn pro and started assessing the various offers. A short while later, representatives of the Ice Follies flew from Los Angeles to Toronto for a final meeting with him—and Don signed with them.

His first couple of years with the Ice Follies were exciting with perhaps the high point coming when he skated a command performance for Queen Elizabeth and had a chat with her later. The kid from Oshawa had come a long way and he worked hard to keep up his world title standards.

The National Film Board of Canada approached Don with the concept of a movie called "King of Blades" and began shooting long sessions while he continued to tour with the show. With the strain of filming sessions, practice sessions and performances increasing daily, he finally broke

Toronto Telegram

Gilbert A. Milne

Presentation to Don from the City of Toronto by Mayor Nathan Phillips. Don's mother watches proudly

Rotary Carnival at Toronto, April 1962. Don with Stanley G. Reid, the producer of the show

Graphic Artists

Donald Jackson joins the Ice Follies. Don and his parents are shown here with Eddie Shipstad, one of the founders of Ice Follies

down physically and became ill with hepatitis. Doctors told him to rest completely. He did, with an aunt in California, but the road back was difficult.

Don found he had to practise more than ever. The extra work served him well, however, when he skated in the World Pro Invitational figure skating competition in Lake Placid. After a typically astounding free skating exhibition, he captured the gold medal.

The extra work he had put in brought a bonus he hadn't foreseen. As often happened, the show's leads had a daily audience at their workouts: the supporting cast. One chorus-line girl took particular delight in watching Don practise, especially noting the way he radiated joy in skating.

Her name was Joanne Diercks. At first she had no romantic designs on him. She had a steady boyfriend back in Arizona and Don was dating Dorothyann Nelson. Don asked Joanne to dinner. She didn't answer at once because she was worried about Don's relationship with Dorothyann. Later, she found out that Don and Dorothyann had decided to stop dating, so Joanne accepted.

Over the next little while, Don and Joanne went out a few times, finding that they got along rather well. When tragedy struck Joanne's family and she had to return home, skaters got together to help pay for her trip. One contributor was Don. He also sent flowers to her upon her return to the show, but later both dated others for a while. Joanne hadn't told him that she had ended her commitment to her boyfriend back home. Their relationship grew and in October, Don proposed marriage. She said yes and they were married in December.

Ice Follies

Ina Bauer, three-time German Champion and world competitor, and Don Jackson skating in Ice Follies

Don stops to take a second look at Jill Shipstad—with Oscar Johnson and Roy Shipstad, the other two founders of Ice Follies

Shortly thereafter, Joanne was forced to retire. After having an operation on her feet, she started skating too soon and her impatience forced her retirement. Don was now into his sixth year with the show, enjoying it immensely, when he received the great news that Joanne was pregnant. However, as had happened to him often before, this good news was followed by near tragedy. Complaining of undue fatigue, Don had been sent to the hospital in Pittsburgh. After two weeks his condition worsened and he couldn't lift his legs. Doctors discovered he had a staphylococcus infection. Joanne, pregnant, was worried. One of Don's eyes was pulsating. A blister on the back of his eyeball left a scar and a lasting blind spot in his vision.

The infection kept Don out of the show for almost three months, including his annual one-month vacation. He and Joanne spent a lot of the time in Arizona with her parents while he regained his strength and started skating once more to get back into shape.

As he regained his skating form, Don went up to Banff, Alberta, to take choreography lessons from Osborne Colson. He had always wanted to have two numbers in the show which would display his athletic world-championship style and allow him to do some character acting. It was in the latter vein that he received help from Colson. Once he had gained sufficient experience, he went to the Ice Follies and asked to have the two numbers included in the show.

Due to illness, Don was absent from the annual contract negotiations. He had not signed for his coming seventh year. Through telephone conversations, he made it clear that he wanted at least a little bit of acting along with his competitive number. Finally the management said okay.

Don Jackson about to be introduced to the Queen Mother. Sjoukje Dijkstra in the background

Mr. and Mrs. Tim Beatty, flanked by Mrs. Billie Mitchell and Donald Knight, who became North American Men's Champion in 1967. Mrs. Mitchell became the first woman president of the Canadian Figure Skating Association

Don with his godson, Donald Frohler, in Prague, 1964

He signed a one-year contract—just about the time the Ice Follies were signing a new Olympic champion, Peggy Fleming.

The final show that season was to be in Madison Square Garden in New York City and was to serve also as a taping for a Peggy Fleming TV special. Peggy's manager offered Don two minutes in the show. He agreed. On that final night in New York, Don dazzled the spectators with two triple salchow jumps in a row plus several of his legendary axels with arms folded across the chest. He felt heartened by the fact that his last public show as a professional had gone perfectly. However, in the dressing room he was informed that the TV segment had been too long. His number was being cut. Only the audience had benefited from what had been one of Don's finest performances.

II

With a home base finally established, Don began to search out ways of putting back some of what he had received from the sport he loved. He was invited to work with Osborne Colson in Banff. It was a team training situation later adopted by the Canadian Figure Skating Association, a first in Canada. Many coaches worked with the skaters simultaneously and exchanged methods of coaching theory. Don welcomed the opportunity and from it embarked upon his own instructional programme.

First to take advantage of Don's availability were amateur clubs across Canada. They were delighted to find Don willing to skate exhibitions at their amateur carnivals and then to follow up with seminars on teaching and train-ing. As his work gained renown, he found himself deluged

Ice Follies

Don's third year with Ice Follies

Ice Follies

Ice Follie

Don on the Mike Douglas show

With Mike Douglas and Debbie Williams from the Ice
Follies Family Act

A skating lesson—trying out a teflon "ice
surface

with requests from countries all over the world. During the next two years he worked with skaters in Australia, Czechoslovakia, Japan and the United States.

But Don's greatest desire was to make a significant contribution to skating in Canada. The amateur carnivals had been a start, but had not been enough. As the early years of the seventies came and went, he worked harder in seminars for clubs across the country. In Toronto he offered advice to the skating schools on training techniques, and also strove to help create new techniques of coaching. All this kept him very busy, along with appearance commitments. He and Joanne had two more sons and a daughter. He was a settled, busy family man, but still he managed to continue to practise an hour a day in order to stay in shape and maintain the unmatched level of skating he had shown for over a decade. And, unexpectedly, he was given once more the chance to remind the skating world of the flaming style that had made him the toast of his time.

III

It was January 18th, 1977. The place was Maple Leaf Gardens in Toronto, and 12,000 spectators were wrapped in momentary blackness.

A voice boomed over the loudspeaker system: "Ice Follies is proud to present in a special guest appearance, our Canadian and World Champion—Donald Jackson!"

To strains from the musical *Mame*, Don sped out onto the ice, his smile once more ear-to-ear. Within thirty seconds he performed three double jumps. He went on and executed more than 15 extremely difficult jumps during his three-and-a-half minute programme.

Ice Follies

Ice Follies

Ice Follies World Premiere in Los Angeles

With Lawrence and Fern Welk

With Herb Alpert and Uschi Keszler

Bob McIntyre

Don stops off at the Broadmoor while on tour with Ice Follies. L to R: Duane Maki, Billy Chapel, David Jenkins, Donald Jackson

But the astounded audience had not seen all. Near the end of the show's second half, he skated again, this time to music from the rock opera *Jesus Christ Superstar*. In his first segment, his jumping had been paramount, but now he exhibited the famous Jackson footwork that had amazed the skating world so many times. His speed was unparalleled. The crowd responded with an ovation when Don executed two double axels in quick succession. The conclusion of his second routine came amid wild cheers. It was clear to anyone: at 36, the King had returned as if he'd never been away. His own enjoyment was even more obvious in the show's finale when Don followed the line grinning and laughing with the audience as he tried to remember a programme he'd only had three days to learn.

In the dressing room, Don reflected on the performance. He questioned only two things: had he done his best? and, had he enjoyed the skating? Both answers: yes. Even though his new boots had been far too stiff he was not tired as he thought he might have been. Why had he come out of retirement? Easy. It was to skate in the show he loved, in the place he loved, and in front of the people he loved. . . .

Sitting with a reporter later, talk turned back to his decision to turn professional. Did he miss the Olympic gold medal that he almost certainly would have won? Sure he missed it—but the decision had been right. After all, he had met Joanne in the show. He might not have done so had he waited three years to sign. Then there was always the chance of injury before the big competition. "I might have sprained my ankle trying to land a quadruple salchow," he said.

A *quadruple salchow*!?!? Yes, Sheldon had already talked

Joanne Diercks advertising her home city, with Mr. Frick

Joanne shown here with Mr. and Mrs. Nelson Rockefeller

with Don before the World Championship about the possibility of landing one when they would have time to work on it after the championship. However, Don downplayed the far-reaching effect of the notion. He said probably he'd never have been able to land it properly.

Yet, one somehow felt that if anyone could have done it, it would be "Me First".

Don meets Joanne

Don and Joanne announce their engagement. Picture
taken backstage at Detroit in November, 1965

Toronto Telegram

The bride and groom with parents looking on

Toronto Telegram

Signing the register

A brief honeymoon—another show in Philadelphia the next day!

Don and Joanne are crowned King and Queen of Winter
—Lake Placid, Christmas, 1967

Orie Damewood

Uschi Keszler, world competitor, and Don—Ice Follies stars

World and Olympic Champion, Peggy Fleming,
joins Ice Follies

Don and Joanne with their first child, Donald Jr., Christmas, 1968

R. Silvester

Don wins the World Men's Professional Championship at Empire Pool, London, April 17th, 1970, for "The Jackson Haines Trophy". On Don's right is runner-up, Paul McGrath of USA; on Don's left is bronze medallist, Michael Edmonds, of Great Britain

British Professional Champion, for the "Embassy Trophy"—April 17th, 1970. Don was first by every judge, and received the only three perfect marks in the championship

Don's first return visit to a world championship in ten years—Calgary, 1972. L to R: Stanislav Zhuk, Soviet coach and former world pairs competitor, Irina Rodnina and Alexei Ulanov, Olympic and World Pairs Champions from the USSR, Donald Jackson

Donald Jr. and Derek get their first skates at St. Gervais, France, where Donald Sr. was teaching and skating shows

Jean Burnier

Don at St. Gervais with Swiss pair champions, Christian and Karin Kuenzle (on the ice). Standing behind the boards is André Calame, one of the founders of the St. Gervais summer competition

Two former world champions meet in the Press Room at the 1973 World's at Bratislava—Don Jackson and Gaby Seyfert—both working for the press in their respective countries

The three top men in the 1962 World's meet again in Bratislava in 1973— Karol Divin, Donald Jackson, Dr. Alain Calmat

A presentation to Donald Jackson by Mayor Mel Lastman of the Borough of North York in Metropolitan **Toronto.**

Don inspects the support for the Don Jackson line of skating boots being hand made in Czechoslovakia.

Don working with Osborne Colson and one of the young skaters at the Toronto Cricket Skating and Curling Club Summer Session, 1977

The Donald Jackson family—Derek, Donald Jr., Michael, Donald Sr., Joanne holding Jeannine

DONALD JACKSON
KING OF BLADES

A List of His Major Awards

Figure Skating Championships

Donald Jackson won the very first figure skating competition he ever entered: the Tonkin Trophy for the Oshawa Skating Club Novice Championship in 1950. During the next five years he competed in many Club and Interclub competitions, nearly always being either winner or runner-up.

1955, January—won the Canadian Junior Men's Championship for the Howard Trophy, held at the Toronto Skating Club—his first time in the Canadian Championships—represented the Minto Skating Club—first in compulsory figures—unanimously first in final results.

1956, March—runner-up to third-time winner Charles Snelling for the Canadian Senior Men's Championship, held at the Galt Figure Skating Club—third in compulsory figures, but pulled up into second place over-all, with four second placings and one third.

1957, February—fourth place in the North American Championship, held at the Genessee Skating Club (Rochester, N.Y.)—represented the Minto Skating Club—fourth place after compulsory figures as well.

1957, February—runner-up to Charles Snelling for the Canadian Senior Men's Championship held at the Winnipeg Winter Club.

1957, March—seventh place in the World Championship held in Colorado Springs—pulled up from tenth place after the compulsory figures—fifth in free skating—final judges' ordinals included one fourth and three sixths.

1958, January—runner-up to Charles Snelling for the Canadian Championship held at the Minto Skating Club (Ottawa)—represented the Oshawa Skating Club—was third in compulsory figures, first in free skating, second over-all, with a first-place ordinal from one of the judges.

1958, February—fourth place in the World Championship held in Paris—pulled up from ninth place after the compulsory figures— second in free skating—final judges' ordinals included a second and a third.

1959, January—won the Canadian Senior Men's Championship for the Minto Cup, held at the Noranda Skating Club—represented the Toronto Cricket Skating and Curling Club—first after compulsory figures—first in free skating—unanimously first in final results.

1959, February—won the North American Men's Championship for the Rogers Trophy, held by the Toronto Cricket Skating and Curling Club—third after compulsory figures—unanimously first over-all.

1959, February—runner-up to third-time winner David Jenkins for the World Championship, held in Colorado Springs—fourth in figures—second in free skating—second over-all.

1960, February—won the Canadian Senior Men's Championship for the second time, held at Wascana Club (Regina)—first in figures, first over-all (unanimously).

1960, February—third place in the Olympics, held at Squaw Valley —fourth place after compulsory figures.

1960, March—runner-up to Alain Giletti for the World Champion- ship, held in Vancouver—second in compulsory figures, unanimously first in free skating, but could not overcome Giletti's 33-point lead in figures—final ordinal included two first placings.

1961, January—won the Canadian Senior Men's Championship for the third time, held at Lachine (Quebec)—unanimous first place.

1961, February—won the North American Men's Championship for the second time, held at the Philadelphia Skating Club and Humane Society—unanimous first place.

1962, February—won the Canadian Senior Men's Championship for the fourth time, held at the Toronto Cricket Skating and Curling Club—unanimous first place—also won the F. Herbert Crispo Memorial Trophy for the best free skating, presented for the first time—also unanimous first place.

1962, March—became the first Canadian in this century to win the Men's World Championship, held in Prague—seven perfect marks received for his free skating program—a record never equalled before or since.

Summary of his major championship placings:

	Senior Canadian	North American	Worlds	Olympics
1956	2	—	*	*
1957	2	4	7	—
1958	2	—	4	—
1959	1	1	2	—
1960	1	—	2	3
1961	1	1	—	—
1962	1	—	1	—

— not held   *not entered

Note that every time Donald won a Canadian or North American Championship his final results showed him to be unanimously in first place.

1965—won World Professional Invitational Championship at Lake Placid (December 22nd-23rd).

1970—won the World *and* British Men's Professional Championships at Empire Pool, Wembley (England) for "The Jackson Haines Trophy" and the "Embassy Trophy" respectively (April 17th). Don was first by every judge, and received the only three perfect marks in the Championship.

Figure Skating Proficiency Tests

Don passed his First Figure Test, eventually, on April 1st, 1951. No April Fool that one! Four years and four months later he passed his

(Canadian) Gold Medal Test in figures and free skating. Subsequently he achieved credit for every North American test available to him at that time, and by September 1961 he had received four gold medals for his efforts—both the figure and dance tests of the Canadian and United States Figure Skating Associations.

Other Awards

1955—Summer—won the Lake Placid Sportsmanship Award. Don is especially proud of this honour because the voting was done by fellow skaters and competitors training there. (September 5th.)

1962—Lou Marsh Trophy—Canada's Outstanding Athlete of the Year.

1962—Honorary Life Membership in the Oshawa Skating Club.

1962—Honorary Life Membership in the Minto Skating Club (Ottawa).

1962—Honorary Life Membership in the Skating Club of New York.

1962—BBC-TV International Athlete of the Year—the "Sportsview International Award" (December 19th).

1962—Canada's Sports Hall of Fame (at the Canadian National Exhibition).

1972—Canadian Amateur Athletic Hall of Fame—Ottawa (December 20th).

1977—Granite Club (Toronto) Hall of Fame (May).

1977—USFSA Figure Skating Hall of Fame—special presentation made by Mr. C. A. DeMore, President of the United States Figure Skating Association, at a joint meeting of the Professional Skating Association of Canada, and the Professional Skaters Guild of America, Toronto, June 4th.

"I doubt if there will ever be such a competitive genius as Jackson on ice again," Dick Button